Teaching Romans Backwards

A STUDY GUIDE TO
READING ROMANS BACKWARDS
BY SCOT MCKNIGHT

Becky Castle Miller

1845BOOKS

Cover and Interior Design by Savanah N. Landerholm

ISBN 978-1-4813-1231-8

To Janet
and all the other women walking like Phoebe today,
carrying the message of Peace
into the Power and Privilege of Empires

CONTENTS

INTRODUCTION

Three years ago, I had no idea what to do with Romans. As a life-long Christian who likes the Bible, I had read Romans, but it felt theologically over my head. Romans was for serious scholars, so the thought of attempting to understand it—much less *teach* it—seemed presumptuous to me, a lay leader in my church. Even a year later, as a new seminary student, it still daunted me. Our cohort at Northern Seminary had a series of four Romans courses with Dr. Scot McKnight in our Master's in New Testament degree plan. The syllabus surprised me: the *first* course covered the *last* chapters of the epistle! Dr. McKnight's plan to teach us the end of the book at the beginning of our classes seemed unconventional to me, but I had learned to trust him as a teacher. "You need to know the context of Romans to interpret it rightly," he told us, "and the context is in chapters twelve to sixteen."

He was right. We started backwards, with Deacon Phoebe in Romans 16:1, performing the letter in the Roman house churches. We considered her targeting in turn the Weak and the Strong as she brought Paul's peace-making into their dinner table conflict. And suddenly Romans started to make sense. God intended to form a new covenant community in Rome, but the ethnic, cultural, and religious struggles between the Jewish and Gentile followers of Jesus were preventing that family kind of unity. Paul wrote for that context, and in light of that context, the letter became clear to me. It was about multiethnic inclusion in the family of God, not about individual salvation disembodied from the church.

For my final paper in that first Romans class, I wrote a piece of biblical fiction, a short story about Phoebe caring for the church in her home, working on a letter with Paul and Timothy, arguing over the wording by lamplight, funding the production, carrying that letter to the Christians in Rome, and presenting it to them in their gatherings. As I worked with the cultural and historical information we learned in class, I envisioned an early church meal through Phoebe's eyes: if people can't even agree on what's lawful to eat, how can they feast together in love? I have included that story in Appendix E of this study guide.

Fast forward a year to our seminary cohort's study trip in Paul's footsteps. We traveled through Turkey and Greece on our way to Italy, visiting the sites of Paul's churches. Dr. McKnight had asked me to bring my story about Phoebe to present during our trip, possibly even in Cenchreae, her home town. I had chosen my clothes for that day very carefully—my empire-waist blue dress and gold-leaf headband were almost normal enough to pass for street clothes but just weird enough to become a costume. After our stop at the Corinth Canal, our Greek tour guide didn't want to sidetrack to Cenchreae. She had a schedule to keep, and the impressive archaeological site and museum at Corinth were more important than the nearly nonexistent ruins of the tiny seaside village of Cenchreae. Dr. McKnight saw my face droop when he told me I might have to read in Corinth instead, so he climbed on the bus and patiently talked the driver into diverting our path south to the Saronic Gulf.

When the bus pulled over onto the dusty shoulder of the highway, my classmates and I poured out of the bus onto a small beach in a cove. To our left, thatched umbrellas dotted the sand, shading sunbathers. To our right, a leaning chain link fence half-heartedly divided the beach, standing between us and rows of rocks poking out of the azure Aegean.

The harbor of Cenchreae to the left of the ruins.

We wandered around the fence to the water's edge, and I lifted my long skirt to keep it dry as I clambered out onto the rocks. They were the outlines of the buildings that used to be waterfront property but were now almost buried under the waves.

Balanced on the remains of a foundation, I raised my hands and lifted my voice to address my classmates gathered on the shore. "Welcome to my home! My name is Phoebe, and I am the deacon of the church here in Cenchreae." And I read them the first half of my story. In a once-in-a-lifetime trip full of profound experiences, this was my highlight.

Becky Castle Miller teaches a tour group about Phoebe in the ruins of Cenchreae, Greece, where Paul likely wrote the letter to the Romans and from where Phoebe likely departed to carry it to Rome.

As we walked back to the bus, our tour guide smiled and approached me. "That was wonderful! I have never seen this before with any group. Now I understand why we needed to come to Cenchreae." Having seen the end result, she understood the whole.

A few days later, my cohort flew to Rome, a much shorter and easier journey than Phoebe must have had. We strolled along the Forum and peered through cracks in the ruins of excavated homes, trying to imagine the early Christians sitting at dinner with Phoebe, anticipating the letter from Paul. As our tour bus careened through traffic heading outside the city walls to the catacombs, I finished telling Phoebe's story. I tried to paint the scenes in the homes of Priscilla and Aquila, Junia and Andronicus, Tryphena and Tryphosa.

What might Herodion have yelled at Phoebe-in-Paul's-stead, offended when she got to chapter 3? At what point in chapter 14 did Urbanus turn red and steamy? What kind of attitude change did their active faith in the Messiah require of each one of them?

Now having studied Romans backwards, starting from the context of lived theology then working back through the letter, I see it differently. It no longer fazes me—it fascinates me. It feels like a letter of pastoral advice from my brother Paul. His words for the multiethnic church in Rome are timely for my multiethnic church in the Netherlands. Our issues of conscience are different, but our lack of sibling welcome at times is the same. Understanding Romans in its context has helped me apply it to my own.

Dr. McKnight decided that *Reading Romans Backwards* needed a study guide to help readers engage with the commentary and to help church leaders and Sunday school teachers present Romans to their students. In my current position on the pastoral staff at my church, I train small group leaders and curious Bible nerds. They have busy lives, and they don't have much experience yet with biblical scholarship, so I've learned how to present serious academics at their level and in the short time they can devote to these side studies. That's what we hope to do with this study guide.

We hope this will bring Romans to life in your context, that teaching Romans backwards will help many Christians learn to love and welcome their siblings in Christ, forging peace in the hearts of empires all over the world today.

HOW TO USE THIS STUDY GUIDE

This study guide is designed to help teachers and students work through *Reading Romans Backwards* in an engaging, interactive way. This guide could be used in a small group, Bible study, Sunday school class, university or seminary class, or even a gathering of friends who want to study Romans together. Though it's not specifically designed for individual study, it could certainly be used that way. I've included a range of learning activities, from simple to complex, so that there are options for all levels of students and various learning styles.

The book is designed for the fifteen-week semester that many American colleges and universities use. Many churches also run small groups, Bible studies, and Sunday school classes in fall and spring sessions that last about fifteen weeks each.

Depending on how you schedule the Lesson Zero introductory material and the Lesson Fifteen exam and conclusion material, your class could run between fourteen and sixteen weeks.

For those who run on shorter trimesters or prefer to move through the book more quickly, I've included a plan for covering the material in eight weeks in Appendix A.

For those using *Reading Romans Backwards* at the university or seminary level as part of a larger course, I've included in Appendix D a list of other books on Romans. You could assign several of these or pull additional readings from them. I focused on books that are readable for non-academics and are not too expensive. Several of these are books that McKnight has used in his series of courses on Romans at Northern Seminary, in which he has, in fact, taught Romans backwards.

BEFORE CLASS

Assign to students the "before class" items. These are listed with check-boxes under each lesson. Before classes, students should complete the selected readings from *Reading Romans Backwards*, the relevant Bible readings, and the Personal Study Questions. Students should come to class each week with these assignments completed in order to be prepared for the Group Discussion Questions and Group Learning Activities.

DURING CLASS

As an instructor, you may want to begin the classroom time by saying what McKnight calls "the Jesus Creed" together with your students. This is something McKnight does at the opening of every seminary class period he teaches in order to focus the learning on the ultimate goal: that through studying the Bible, student and teacher alike would come to love God and love their neighbors. (See Scot McKnight's book *The Jesus Creed* for more information.)

Hear, O Israel, the Lord our God, the Lord is one. Love the Lord your God with all your heart, with all your soul, with all your mind, and with all your strength. The second is this: love your neighbor as yourself. There is no commandment greater than these. (Taken from Matthew 22:37-40 and Mark 12:30-31)

Depending on your knowledge, experience, and the length of your class period together, you could write lectures that expound on the topics covered in the lessons. The websites listed in each lesson could help with these.

Consider beginning with a review of the week's readings so students can discuss their impressions and ideas in a free-flowing way. The Main Takeaway and Chapter Summary sections could help guide your review.

Choose from the Group Discussion Questions and Group Learning Activities to structure the classroom time. Read through these ahead of the class time to check whether you need to prepare or bring any supplies. Many of these are activities McKnight has done in his seminary classes or I have done with my international church.

You can use the Quiz Questions for weekly quizzes, compile them together for midterm or final exams, or use them as a basis for a weekly review. The answers are in Appendix B. Appendix C has suggested essay topics in case you want to assign papers during the course.

Instructors may want to end the class time by praying the Lord's Prayer together with the students, which is how McKnight ends his classes. The repetition of the opening and closing Scripture recitations forms a liturgy that helps shape students over time into focusing on Jesus's prayers, teachings, and priorities.

AFTER CLASS

Remind students to do the follow-up Bible study homework for additional biblical learning. Assign the following week's readings and questions.

PRE-READING QUESTIONS

1. What do you know about the book of Romans?

2. What experiences, if any, have you had in reading Romans (forward) in the past?

3. Off the top of your head, what do you think the book of Romans is about?

4. What do you hope to gain from this study?

LESSON ZERO

THE FIRST CLASS

BEFORE CLASS

❑ No pre-work required

This first class is optional. You could begin your first session together with Lesson One—however, if you do that, you'll need to assign the reading for that lesson to be finished before the first class. Some students will find it easier to move into the material more slowly by beginning with this introductory class.

If you do an introductory class session, here are some suggestions.

GROUP LEARNING ACTIVITY SUGGESTIONS

Get to know each other. Introduce yourselves and share your story and the interest that brought you to this class.

Discuss the pre-reading questions.

Watch together a one-hour webinar by Scot McKnight on reading Romans backwards. In the first 30 minutes (starting at about 4 minutes into the video and ending at about the 34-minute mark), McKnight gives a brief overview of the interpretive history of Romans, why he teaches Romans backwards, and how he interprets each main section (12–16, 9–11, 1–4, and 5–8). This is a good overview that could help prepare the students to read the book with the big picture in mind. It can also be helpful for people to hear and see an author on video before they read, so that they can better "hear" the words of the book in the author's voice. That video is here: http://bit.ly/WebinarRRB.

Take time in class to turn to Appendix E and each silently read the story "Our Sister Phoebe" to get an overview of the course content in the format of an imaginative narrative. Discuss the story together. Alternately, you could assign students to read the story on their own before or after this first class session.

Explain the format of the study guide and the plan for the class. Pass out a syllabus or course calendar if you make one. Assign the reading and personal study questions for the following week.

LESSON ONE

PREFACE, INTRODUCTION, CHAPTER 1

BEFORE CLASS

- ❏ Read the Table of Contents
- ❏ Read the Preface (3 pages)
- ❏ Read the Introduction (3 pages)
- ❏ Read Romans 16:1-16
- ❏ Read Chapter 1 (3 pages)
- ❏ Answer the Personal Study Questions

MAIN TAKEAWAY

Romans is a letter written to the small group of Jesus-followers in Rome, their number made up of Jews and Gentiles, poor and rich, slaves and free, women and men.

The context for all the theology in the early parts of the letter is given at the *end of the letter*, so we read Romans *backwards* to situate the theology better in its multiethnic Roman house church context.

Power and Privilege were at play in the Roman culture, causing tension between the Strong and the Weak in the churches. Paul wanted the followers of Jesus in Rome to turn from the dominant cultural forces and instead embrace Peace and each other.

Terms and Definitions

Introduction

Privilege	In general, Privilege is the collection of benefits a culture gives a person or people group that helps them succeed more easily. Privilege isn't earned; it is simply possessed, and it comes from a person's innate attributes and the value the culture places on those attributes. Cultural power is usually given to the privileged. For the Strong in Romans, their Privilege is their status as the majority, as Romans and as non-Jews. For the Weak, their Privilege is their consciousness of being God's elect and their sense of moral superiority for keeping the Torah.
Power	Power is the strength held by those at the top of a hierarchy and is wielded over and against the people further down the hierarchy. Power gives access to instruments of coercion. Power itself is neutral but leans toward being misused to abuse the ones without power.
Peace	For Christians, Peace is created in Christ. It is a countercultural steadiness that opposes the ethnocentrism of Roman elites and their Privilege. It is the unity in relationships between people who are different, and that unity comes through the Spirit, not through human force. In Romans, the Peace needs to come into the relationships between the Weak and the Strong. Peace tempers Power in the direction of goodness and Christlikeness.
Pax Romana	Latin for "Roman Peace." It refers to a stable period in the Roman Empire between approximately 27 BCE and 180 CE. During the *Pax Romana*, life was good for those with Privilege and Power but not so good for those without status. Paul's idea of Peace, in contrast, is good news for everyone.
Via vitae	Latin for "way of life." Here it is used to talk about a way to live out theology in the life of the church body.

Chapter 1

Cursus honorum	Latin for "course of honor" or "path toward honor." Here it is used to explain the cultural norm in Roman society to advance, on the basis of one's social status and Privilege, in pursuing public honor, glory, and fame.

Chapter Summaries
Preface

- We can understand chapters 1 through 11 of Romans better by looking first at chapters 12 through 16. This is what McKnight calls "reading Romans backwards: first, Romans 12–16, then 9–11, then 1–8" (ix).
- Many approaches to interpreting Romans see it as a theological treatise rather than a contextualized letter to house churches in Rome. The context is first-century Rome under Emperor Nero, and the timing is when Paul was planning to carry the good news of Jesus on a further missionary journey to Spain.
- Two main ways of reading Romans emerge in the scholarship. One sees Romans as talking about individual salvation. The other sees Romans as talking about the church and how those in the church can be reconciled into a fellowship of different siblings. McKnight's approach is the second, focusing on intra-church relationships.
- In looking at the themes of Privilege, Power, and Peace, this approach focuses on hearing Romans through "the (imagined) ears of the Weak and Strong" (x).

Introduction

- Church people today still grapple with the same issues Paul tackles in Romans: "the inability of the Privileged and the Powerful to embody the gospel's inclusive demand and include the Disprivileged and the Disempowered. The mirror of this issue is the Disempowered claiming their own kind of Privilege and Power" (xiii).
- Power and Privilege lead to injustice, while the gospel of Peace deconstructs and denies both to bring God's justice.
- The practical advice for living out theology in the day-to-day life of the house churches that we find in Romans 12–16 is not an inconsequential add-on to the letter. Rather, it is the point of the letter. Romans 1–11 is the theological explanation that undergirds the pastoral advice of Romans 12–16.

Chapter 1: Phoebe—The Face of Romans (16:1-2)

- "Letters in Paul's world were the embodied, inscripted presence of the letter writer, in this case Paul. He chooses a woman to embody his letter, which means the face of Paul is experienced as the face of Phoebe" (3).

- Paul calls Phoebe "sister." This is an example of the way Paul's frequent sibling language creates a new social order. The Roman world assigned people status based on their biological family, their wealth, or their success. By calling other Christians in the church "siblings," Paul makes them family and reorients people's basis for status on their being "in Christ"—and in Christ, they all have equal status. This disrupts the Roman ideas about Privilege and Power.
- Phoebe is a deacon, which can mean "servant," yet in the churches, it could mean an officially recognized ministry or office. Because Paul connects Phoebe with the church in Cenchreae, it seems she held a ministry leadership position there. It's possible she is the host, the patron (the one who funds), and the leader of that church.
- Phoebe is a benefactor—a wealthy person who financially provides for people—for Paul and many others.
- Paul commends Phoebe to the Romans in a way that indicates she both *carried* and *performed* the letter.
- "... reading as performance included gestures at the right time and to the right segment of the audience (when Phoebe read "Strong" or "Weak," she looked them in the eye, or, if she thought they needed it, the opposing group in the eye!); inflection of the voice (here pastoral, there admonishing, here softening, and there exhorting) ... We start here, then, with our reading of Romans: with the face of Phoebe, in our presence, performing the letter in such a way that each person in the churches senses Paul's presence" (5).

Group Discussion Questions

Turn back to the Pre-Reading Questions you answered at the beginning of this study guide. Discuss them together (unless you already did this in your first class session together).

What were your thoughts about Romans before starting this study, and how have your thoughts changed already?

How are church offices or ministry leadership positions designated in your church? Does your tradition have deacons? Do women like Phoebe serve as deacons in your denomination?

What kind of work do female and male deacons do in your church?

Look at the list of names in Romans 16. Imagine being in the room as Phoebe read the letter. How would you feel to be greeted by name by Paul?

GROUP LEARNING ACTIVITY SUGGESTIONS

Look at a map of the Mediterranean in the first century and trace Phoebe's possible journey routes from Cenchreae to Rome (see page 3 of *Reading Romans Backwards* for possibilities). One such map is in the Resources section below.

Look online for recent pictures of the Port of Cenchreae. The shoreline has shifted, but some ruins still stick up from the water.

Note on a map how close Cenchreae is to Corinth and imagine the Christians in Cenchrea also having read Paul's letters to the Corinthians. If Phoebe had heard the letters to Corinth, what might she have thought of them (and of Paul)?

Make name tags with the names from Romans 16, one for each person in the class. If the class is bigger than the list of names, add in name tags with typical Roman names. Designate a woman in the class to be Phoebe. She can stand before the class and perform a reading of Romans 16, looking at each person in the class as she reads out the greeting of their character name from the chapter. Ask the students to save their name tags for next week, because they will use them again.

Name tags for a first-century house church meeting at a church retreat. We set it in Corinth, so Erastus, Gaius, and Phoebe were among those in attendance. Every person had a character—slaves, Gentiles, Jews, people of various socio-economic levels and professions—to show the makeup of a Roman household church according to Peter Oakes. We worshipped with an early liturgy, took up a collection for the poor, then went to dinner together where we shared communion as part of our love feast.

RESOURCES FOR FURTHER INFORMATION

- Map of the Roman empire in the first century
  https://www.bible-history.com/maps/romanempire/
- Beverly Gaventa's lectures on Romans 16
    + "Listening to Phoebe Read Romans"
      http://bit.ly/PhoebeReadsRomans
    + "Reading Romans with Junia and Her Sisters"
      http://bit.ly/JuniaAndSisters
- Paula Gooder's book *Phoebe: A Story* takes readers into a creative
  exploration of Phoebe's story, the tensions in the house churches in
  Rome, the reception to Paul's letter, and his mission to Spain. This
  would make excellent supplemental reading during the course to help
  students truly enter the context of the letter to the Romans.

FURTHER BIBLE STUDY

Acts 18. This chapter tells the beginning of the story of Paul's friendship
with Priscilla and Aquila, whom he greets in Romans 16. Note the location
Paul meets them, the location he has his hair cut to show his vow, and the
location he leaves them. What type of job does Paul share in common with
them? What kind of ministry work does this couple do together at the end of
the chapter? How do they use their home for ministry? What do you imagine
their life looked like once they returned to Rome?

PERSONAL STUDY QUESTIONS—LESSON ONE

Table of Contents

What titles does McKnight give to the four sections of Romans?
> Romans 12–16:
> Romans 9–11:
> Romans 1–4:
> Romans 5–8:

Introduction

On page xiv, what does McKnight argue that Romans 12–16 reveals?

What does Romans 9–11 reveal?

What does Romans 1–8 reveal?

Chapter 1

List four things Paul says about Phoebe.

> 1.
> 2.
> 3.
> 4.

Quiz Questions—Lesson One

1. Which is NOT a major theme in *Reading Romans Backwards*?

   A. Peace
   B. Power
   C. Prosperity
   D. Privilege

2. Who carried Paul's letter to the Roman house churches?

   A. Priscilla
   B. Phoebe
   C. Paul
   D. Peter

True or False

3. Claudius was the emperor of Rome when Paul wrote his letter.

4. Paul uses the language of siblings to talk about relationships in the church.

5. Romans is a theological treatise about individual salvation.

LESSON TWO

CHAPTER 2

BEFORE CLASS

❑ Read Romans 16:1-16
❑ Read Chapter 2 (8 pages)
❑ Answer the Personal Study Questions

MAIN TAKEAWAY

The Jesus followers in Rome were both Jewish and Gentile, but the Gentiles held the majority position. The believers gathered in homes for household church meetings. There were probably five small communities of Christians in first-century Rome, and they mostly lived in poor areas of the city.

TERMS AND DEFINITIONS

Chapter 2

Numismatic	Relating to coins.
Christoform	Being shaped or formed into the likeness of Jesus.

CHAPTER SUMMARIES

Chapter 2: The Greetings and the House Churches of Rome (16:3-16)

- By looking at the list of names in Romans 16 as well as considering archaeological details, scholars estimate that there were likely five separate house churches in Rome. Phoebe may have read the letter to each gathering separately—the entire letter, five times!
- Based on house sizes and household makeup of the time, scholars estimate each church had at maximum 40 members. Doing the math (40 × 5), we can estimate the number of Christians in Rome at 200 or fewer. This is in a city of over a million people.

- Based on archaeological and literary evidence, it's possible to determine where the early Roman house churches gathered in the city. These were immigrant-heavy areas and areas of low income, which means the followers of Jesus in Rome were mostly poor, though there were several high-status, wealthy people among them.

  + "the port area of the Tiber called the **Trastevere** (trast-EH-ver-eh)"
  + "on a main road through the heart of first-century Rome called **Via Appia**"
  + "in an area called the **Aventine**, where more and more senators were forming their homes . . . but the evidence is not as abundant."
  + "North and slightly west of the Forum was Mars Field, and along its eastern side is the **Via Lata/Flaminia**" (8, emphasis added)

- The early Christian movement in Rome came out of the synagogues and was mostly Jewish. Acts 18 mentions the disturbance among Jews under Claudius which led the Emperor to kick the Jews (possibly specifically the Jewish followers of Jesus) out of Rome. This sent Priscilla and Aquila out to where they met Paul. When young Nero became emperor, he allowed the Jews back in.

- When the expelled Jewish Christians returned to Rome, they found the churches changed. The Gentile Christians had developed a Christian culture that no longer included observing the Torah. The power balance of the early church had turned upside down. Originally the Roman church had been majority Jewish, and now it was majority Gentile. This created tensions around Power and Privilege.

- The make-up of a house church was basically the make-up of a household: the householder, family members, workers, dependents, and slaves. The various households listed in Romans 16 are distinguishable by designations like "house," "family," and "with them." The groups are generally identified with the name of the householder. Picture a living room or a kitchen table and imagine lounging after dinner with friends to hear the letter from Paul.

- The process of Bible translation has included Latinizing names, which has hidden the variety of Greek, Latin, and Jewish names in the list. The variety of names also indicates the variety of languages spoken in the church gatherings.

- "Women's leadership at Rome is obvious: Prisca, Mary, Junia, Tryphaena and Tryphosa (perhaps sisters), Persis, Rufus' mother, Julia, Nereus' sister, as well as the sisters in the household of Asyncritus. Prisca—known to Luke as Priscilla (the diminutive form)—was an itinerant missionary church planter" (13).
- Part of Peace for Paul is unity in diversity. We can see the need for that unity in this diverse fellowship: people of different social statuses, people of different sexes, people of different language and ethnic groups.

Wealthy terraced homes in Ephesus showing the insides of houses where rich Romans lived. Notice the variety of decorations on the walls and floors made of paint and tile.

An indoor/outdoor courtyard in Pompeii. The extended living space could have comfortably fit 50 people or more. Perhaps wealthy Christians in Rome hosted Phoebe to read Paul's letter in a villa like this.

Group Discussion Questions

Based on the information on pages 8–9 of *Reading Romans Backwards*, work together to create a sketch of the lives of the early Roman Christians. List the areas where they might have lived, then list the occupations they might have held, then list the types of homes they might have lived in.

Look at page 10 of *Reading Romans Backwards* and work together to list the possible "members" of a typical Roman house church. Then describe their meeting space.

Group Learning Activity Suggestions

Look at a map of Rome in the first century and locate the areas where house churches might have gathered.

Try to sort out the various house churches and their members. Draw five circles on a piece of paper or a white board and include in each circle the likely members of each gathering.

Pull up on a screen in the classroom the computer renderings of wealthy Roman villas. The URL is in the Resources section below. Look at them together and discuss how Christian gatherings in the homes of rich or high-status benefactors might have looked. How do you think this differed from the meetings in poorer homes and apartments?

Make three columns on a white board or paper and caption them "Greek names," "Latin names," and "Jewish names." Turn to page 12 of *Reading Romans Backwards* to see the information about the names. Ask the students to take their name tags from the last class and stick them on the paper in the right columns.

Use stickers or a marker to distinguish the name tags of the prominent slaves and women in the Roman house churches (see page 13 of *Reading Romans Backwards*).

Resources for Further Information

- Computer-rendered images of Roman villas
  http://bit.ly/RomanVillas

Further Bible Study

❑ Galatians 3:26-29. How do these verses relate to Paul's message of Peace among siblings to the Roman Christians?

Phoebe may have met with the churches in apartments like these, or in even poorer areas of Rome. This is the Insula dell'Ara Coeli. Archaeologists think this apartment block originally had five stories with shops on the ground floor. Priscilla and Aquila could have set up their leatherworking business and lived upstairs, hosting their church in their shop.

PERSONAL STUDY QUESTIONS—LESSON TWO

Chapter 2

What surprised you in the background information about the early Christians of Rome?

How does a Roman house church differ from your current experience of church?

Quiz Questions—Lesson Two

1. Where in Rome did the Christians likely live?

   A. Trevi, Aventina, Via Appia, Forum
   B. Trastevere, Via Appia, Aventine, Via Lata/Flaminia
   C. Mars Field, Vatican, Fontana, Aventine
   D. Vatican, Trastevere, Serpentina, Forum

2. Who was NOT a prominent Christian woman greeted in Romans 16?

   A. Mary
   B. Tryphena
   C. Junia
   D. Susanna

3. In what year did Claudius expel the Jewish believers from Rome?

   A. 49
   B. 48
   C. 51
   D. 50

True or False

4. The Jesus-followers in Rome at the time Paul wrote his letter were mostly Gentile.

5. The number of Christians in Rome in the first century was likely over 200.

LESSON THREE

BEFORE CLASS

- ❏ Read Romans 14:1–15:13
- ❏ Read Chapter 3 (9 pages)
- ❏ Read Romans 12:14-21 and 13:1-10
- ❏ Read Chapter 4 (2 pages)
- ❏ Answer the Personal Study Questions

MAIN TAKEAWAY

The two main groups discussed in Romans 14–15 are the Weak and the Strong, who are set in intense conflict with each other. The Weak are Jewish followers of Jesus who observe the Torah, and the Strong are Gentile followers of Jesus who are not Torah observant. Privilege and Power lead to tension between the groups, and Paul encourages them toward mutual respect, unity, and Peace as siblings.

TERMS AND DEFINITIONS

Chapter 3

Halakhic	Relating to the halakha, which is the collection of official rulings on implementing the Law of Moses. Halakha oversees applying the commandments to daily life.
Gentile inclusion	God made a covenant with Abraham promising to bless all the nations of the earth (the Gentiles) through Abraham's family (the Israelites/Jews). All along, God intended to bring Gentiles into the covenant people. Paul's work as the apostle to the Gentiles was focused on including Gentiles in the church, the new covenant family of God.

Equestrians	While this word now means someone skilled at riding horses, in first-century Rome, *equites* were high status members of the ruling class. The term came from those who served in the cavalry, but by the first century, it was mostly a political vocation.
Dunatoi	Those who have power.
A-dunatoi	Those who do not have power.

Chapter 4

Zealot	A member of a Jewish group who believed God should be their only ruler. They acted in zealous ways, modeled after God's own zeal, to resist the Roman Empire.

CHAPTER SUMMARIES

Chapter 3: Strong and Weak (14:1–15:13)

- The Strong and the Weak are the big characterizations in Romans 14 and 15. They could be literary constructs Paul is using, but it's much more likely they are real people groups within the churches.
- In general, the Weak are the Jewish believers who follow the Torah and the Strong are the Gentile believers who do not follow the Torah. Some are "stronger" or "weaker" than others, and some probably fall into an undecided or neutral position. They may not be solely divided along Jew/Gentile lines, but this seems to be the majority division.
- Paul's mission was to plant churches of unified believers, taking mixed groups and helping them find peace in fellowship. One of the most common sources of tension in these new churches was between Jewish believers and Gentile believers.
- Paul is likely talking specifically to Jewish followers of Jesus, not to all Jews.
- We can sort out what Paul means by Weak and Strong by looking at these terms not only in Romans but also in 1 Corinthians, which he wrote around the same time. Paul likely wrote Romans from Corinth or nearby Cenchreae.
- McKnight concludes that the Weak are Jewish believers, based on several factors: there are both Jewish and Gentile names in Romans 16, but Gentiles are the majority; Jews were known in Rome for their dietary restrictions; Paul's concern with Jewish-Gentile relations shows up in every section of Romans; Paul concludes the argument

in this section by quoting the Old Testament on Gentile inclusion; and the circumstances of Jewish believers returning to the Gentile-dominant Roman house churches at this time would naturally lead to tension between the groups.

- The conflict between the groups is vehement. The Strong disdain the Weak, looking down on them as lowly and worthless. The Weak take on a god-like role of judging and condemning the Strong.
- This is not just a theological disagreement. This is a disagreement of lived theology, and it's ripping apart this faith community.
- Because some of the main conflicts are about food laws, this makes shared meals between the two groups almost impossible.
- Privilege shows up here in both the Weak (the Privilege of being the covenant owners) and the Strong (the Privilege of holding higher social status in Roman life).
- Power shows up here in the Strong, who have social and cultural Power and probably also wealth. Paul wants them to welcome those without Power, meaning they should use their Power to *empower* their weaker siblings in Christ, not to further *disempower* them.
- Paul seems to see himself as being among the Strong, or on the side of the Strong. However, he does not expect everyone to come to his same conclusions. He allows space for all to live out their own convictions, as long as they do it in peace.
- "The operative terms for Paul . . . are *Welcome one another to the table as siblings!* The whole letter is found in that imperative" (23).

Chapter 4: Zealotry (12:14-21; 13:1-7, 8-10)

- When Paul speaks of civil order and taxation, he seems to be targeting the Weak, the Jewish believers who might have been resisting taxation in the tradition of zealotry.
- Paul himself was a Zealot, so he recognizes the temptation toward zealotry in the Weak.
- The Weak might have been resisting taxation as a form of protest, frustrated by their difficult lot in life when they returned to Rome.

The temple to Apollo in Corinth. Priscilla and Aquila lived and worked in Corinth after being expelled from Rome.

The faint pie-shaped etching in the stone in front of this shop in Ephesus was an early form of the ICTHYS, a mark that distinguished Christian locations so believers could find each other. Priscilla and Aquila could have worked in a shop like this when they lived in Ephesus before returning to Rome.

The theater in Ephesus.

The library in Ephesus.

Group Discussion Questions

Before you read these chapters in *Reading Romans Backwards*, what were your thoughts on the Weak and the Strong in Romans 14–15?

Do you think Paul was among the Strong or among the Weak? Why?

If you are willing, share the personal study answers you wrote about how Privilege and Power play out in your church community.

Consider how you view Christians who have different convictions from you. In your thoughts or words, have you shown disdain or judgment toward them? OR Think about how other Christians have judged or disdained you for your different convictions. Share your experiences, if you are willing.

What were your thoughts about Zealots before you read these chapters? Would you have thought of Paul as a Zealot?

What are forms of resistance to governmental power that your church tradition approves of? What forms of resistance are frowned upon? Paul likely wrote to the Romans in the early part of Nero's reign, before the emperor began severely persecuting the Christians. Do you think Paul might have written the section about obeying the governing authorities differently if he had written it later?

Group Learning Activity Suggestions

Think about this class or your church. Who has Power? OR Who are the *dunatoi* and the *a-dunatoi*? Consider social, ethnic, racial, linguistic, financial, gender, and denominational differences. Make two columns on a white board or sheet of paper and label them *dunatoi* and the *a-dunatoi*. Fill them in with the class's answers. How do those power differentials lead to conflict?

Watch the short video about keeping kosher today (the modern practice of Jewish food laws). The URL is in the Resources section below. Discuss the quote that begins around 54 seconds: "This may well have been part of what God had in mind as it makes it more difficult for practicing Jews to socialize with those who do not share the same religion."

Create a list together regarding issues in churches today that are *adiaphora*—a Greek term meaning indifferent, which is used in theological discussions to refer to matters of conscience. When there is no clear biblical or moral teaching for or against an issue, it is up to the conviction of each Christian how they will practice. What issues would your class put on a list of topics (nonessentials of faith) about which Christians can and do disagree?

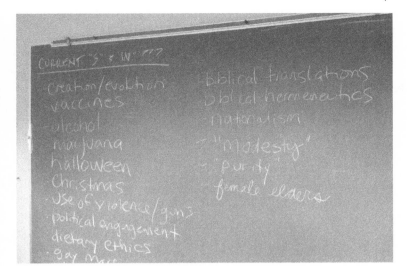

A list from one of Scot McKnight's Romans classes in which students listed diaphora/adiaphora *issues in the church today—the issues that might divide the Strong and the Weak today.*

RESOURCES FOR FURTHER INFORMATION

- Video about kosher kitchens
  http://bit.ly/KeepKosherToday
- Jewish source about halakha
  http://www.jewfaq.org/halakhah.htm
- Britannica article on Zealots
  https://www.britannica.com/topic/Zealot
- Scot McKnight has a podcast called Kingdom Roots. One of his episodes is about Zealots. *Kingdom Roots Podcast Episode 85: Zealots Then and Now.* You can find it on most podcast services.
- *Jesus Creed* blog post by Scot McKnight on Zealots
  http://bit.ly/JesusCreedZealots

FURTHER BIBLE STUDY

❏ 1 Corinthians 8. Read Paul's more specific discussion on food and conscience in this message to the Corinthian believers regarding meat sacrificed to idols. He talks about the Weak here as well.

❏ Galatians 1:13-14, Philippians 3:4-6, Acts 22:2-5. See Paul's references to his zeal and his practice of religion before his encounter with Jesus.

PERSONAL STUDY QUESTIONS—LESSON THREE

Chapter 3

List the points about the Weak on the bottom of page 21 of *Reading Romans Backwards*.

List the points about the Strong on the bottom of page 21.

What is added to the previous definition of the Weak on the bottom of page 25?

Who in your culture has Privilege?

Who in your culture has Power?

How do Privilege and Power play out in your church community?

Chapter 4

Who do you see as the Zealots of modern Christianity?

How do you view resisting the governing authorities as a part of faith practice?

QUIZ QUESTIONS—LESSON THREE

1. The arguments between the Strong and the Weak in Romans 14–15 have to do with

    A. Food laws, holy days, circumcision
    B. Food laws
    C. Food laws, Sabbath
    D. Food laws, vegetarianism, circumcision

2. Which of these is NOT a trait of the Weak?

    A. Jewish believers
    B. Attend synagogue
    C. Do not keep the Torah
    D. Judge the Gentiles

3. Which of these is a trait of the Strong?

    A. Jewish believers
    B. Keep Torah
    C. Do not follow Jesus
    D. Have social status in Rome

True or False

4. Paul's mission was to plant churches made of Jewish believers in Jesus.

5. Paul was a Pharisee and a Zealot.

LESSON FOUR

CHAPTER 5, CHAPTER 6, CHAPTER 7A

BEFORE CLASS

- ❑ Read Romans 14:7-9 and 15:3, 5, 7
- ❑ Read Chapter 5 (2 pages)
- ❑ Read Romans 12:1-2
- ❑ Read Chapter 6 (5 pages)
- ❑ Read Romans 12:3-8 and 16:17-20
- ❑ Read Chapter 7, pages 35–38 (4 pages)
- ❑ Answer the Personal Study Questions

MAIN TAKEAWAY

The central idea of Paul's lived theology for the Roman house churches is Christoformity: becoming like Jesus through the power of the Holy Spirit. As each person becomes more like Jesus, the community will shift from being driven by Power and Privilege to being identified with Peace. As each Christian becomes more Christoform, this will show in the way they are oriented toward or focused on God and other people in the church.

TERMS AND DEFINITIONS

Chapter 5

Quotidian	Everyday, common, daily
Dialectical relationship	Two or more ideas or perspectives in dialogue or discourse with each other. Here it is used to mean that "lived theology" and "theology" are in conversation with each other throughout Romans.
Christoformity	the process of being conformed to Christ.

Chapter 6

Embodied Visible or tangible in a human body. Embodied theology is lived theology—not just theology of ideas but theology of action.

Chapter 7

Praxis Putting ideas into practice instead of just leaving them theoretical. Taking what one learns in religion and actively living it out.

CHAPTER SUMMARIES

Chapter 5: Christoformity—Paul's Vision for a Lived Theology of Peace (14:7-9; 15:3, 5, 7)

- The Christians in Rome knew and lived the context into which Paul was writing. A lived theology for that precise context is Paul's goal for the letter.
- The lived theology ideas are spread throughout the section of Bible text (chapters 12–16). In the next few chapters of *Reading Romans Backwards*, McKnight groups Paul's lived theology ideas into several consolidated themes to better explore them.
- "The central idea [of Romans 12–16] is Christoformity, and it finds expression in an embodied God orientation, a Body-of-Christ orientation, and a public orientation. The result of Christoformity for lived theology is that Power and Privilege are turned toward Peace in the heart of the empire" (27).
- ". . . because of union with Christ, the Roman Christians are not to seek their own life but to seek the life of God-in-Christ for the redemption of others" (28).
- The heart of Paul's theology is Jesus—entering into his life and following his example. Paul's instructions to the Romans flow from the model of Jesus. Christians should live to the Lord, die to the Lord, please others rather than themselves for the Lord, and welcome others in the Lord.

Chapter 6: Christoformity Is Embodied God Orientation (12:1-2)

- Two aspects of embodied God orientation are sacrifice and prayer.
- Six life-changing points about embodied sacrifice:

1. God's mercy/compassion/goodness to the undeserving, both Weak and Strong, enables their sacrifice.
2. This is a new form of sacrifice because it is no longer a tangible object given to gods, but it is the very actions of life. What Christians *do* is the sacrifice.
3. "Spiritual worship" isn't ethereal but rather means that "a gospel-shaped life *is* their worship" (30).
4. The sacrifice is holy, meaning that every part of their lives is devoted to God.
5. Their sacrifice is found in being transformed by the Spirit instead of conformed to the world, meaning the way of the empire. For both Strong and Weak, conformity to empire showed up in the way they derided each other.
6. The sacrifice involves having their minds transformed, bringing them into one mind together in Christ.

- "To turn to God, to embody a life that is sacrificial worship, is to turn from the way of Rome, to turn to Christoformity" (31).
- Six mind-blowing points about prayer:

  1. Paul writes out his prayers in the letter in several places. Imagine the listeners assuming postures of prayer during these parts of Phoebe's reading and joining in Paul's prayers.
  2. Paul's prayers describe attributes of God.
  3. His prayers ask God to give the Romans Christians godly traits like joy, Peace, and hope.
  4. Paul asks the Romans Christians to pray intercessory prayers for him.
  5. The benedictory prayer in Romans 16:25-27 seems to indicate the theme of the whole letter: the inclusion of faithful Gentiles.
  6. Paul's prayers are Trinitarian: to the Father, through the Son, in the Spirit.

Chapter 7: Christoformity Is Embodied Body-of-Christ Orientation (12:3-8; 14–15; 16:17-20)

- God orientation is not individualistic or mystical—it is an embodied life lived together in fellowship with other people.
- There are five earth-shattering themes on lived theology for the Roman Christians: body life, generosity, peace and unity, tolerance, and welcoming to the table.

Body Life

- "To live an embodied life for God is to live with other bodies in the Body of Christ" (35).
- Both Weak and Strong were being *superminded*, thinking of themselves too highly and as better than the other group. Paul tells them that, instead, they should think of themselves as equally important members of the body, according to the gifts the Spirit gave each of them.
- Paul positions the church as an alternate body politic in which actual Peace can be achieved.
- ". . . each gift is something practiced or done, not something owned or possessed" (36). The gifts are given to both Weak and Strong for the benefit of the whole gathered body.

Generosity

- Paul's mission drives his ideas of generosity. As apostle to the Gentiles, he collected funds from the Gentile believers to bring to the poor people of the church in Jerusalem, and he believed those funds would be accepted by the Jewish believers, meaning that the Jewish believers would see that offering as kosher/clean/acceptable.
- Paul acknowledged the church in Jerusalem as the "mother church," and he believed the Gentile believers benefitted from God's covenant with the Jews which now extended to the Gentiles. The Gentile offering he collected was a way of reciprocating gifts to the Jerusalem church.
- "God's gift prompts reciprocal giving to others" (38).
- Christian generosity to each other was a way of achieving care for the poor and economic justice.

Group Discussion Questions

When you pray, how do you address God? How does this compare or contrast with the way Paul addresses his prayers?

Which of the points about embodied sacrifice most stood out to you and why?

How do you view giving offerings to your church? How does this section on generosity affect your thoughts?

GROUP LEARNING ACTIVITY SUGGESTIONS

Read Paul's prayers out loud and invite the class to take postures of prayer (standing with arms raised, sitting with hands folded, kneeling, prostrate on the ground) as you all make these prayers your own. References: Romans 15:13; 16:20; and 16:25-27

Read Romans 12:6-8 out loud, regarding spiritual gifts in the church. Ask three students to read these three other passages about gifts: 1 Corinthians 12:4-11; Ephesians 4:11-13; 1 Peter 4:10-11. Make a list together of all the various gifts mentioned. Which are repeated in different passages?

McKnight wrote, "the gifts Paul mentions in his various listings are shaped by the needs of particular congregations" (37). Discuss this—what do you think this meant in practice in Paul's churches? What gifts do you see a need for in your church today? Take time to pray together that God would empower people in your church with those gifts for the good of the whole church.

Ask a student to read Romans 15:18-29 about Paul's missionary work and his planned trip to Spain. Look on a map of the first-century Mediterranean—there is a URL to one in the Resources section below. Locate all the places mentioned in the Bible text. Guess together about Paul's possible planned routes from Jerusalem to Rome and then on to Spain.

Consider how you and the class could serve poor Christians and act toward economic justice. Is there an organization or nonprofit or project or charity that one of your students is passionate about and can share about with the class? Decide together as a group whom you want to serve with a financial gift. For the rest of your class periods, bring money for that offering, remembering Paul's twenty-year-long collection for the poor in Jerusalem. At the end of the course, add up the amount given and give the gift as a class.

RESOURCES FOR FURTHER INFORMATION

- Grace/Gift—John Barclay. The author of *Paul and the Gift*, a major work on re-understanding grace in Paul's writing, made this short video which highlights some aspects of first-century gift giving, God's generosity, and Gentile inclusion.
  http://bit.ly/BarclayGrace
- Map of the Roman provinces in 117 CE.
  http://bit.ly/RomanEmpire117
- Did Paul go to Spain? This URL has quotes from early-church sources claiming that Paul did, indeed, make that trip.
  http://bit.ly/PaultoSpain

FURTHER BIBLE STUDY

- ❏ <u>Philippians 2:6-11; Colossians 1:15-20.</u> Paul seems to be quoting two existing hymns of the church.
- ❏ <u>Galatians 2:1-10; Acts 11:27-30; 1 Corinthians 16:1-4; 2 Corinthians 8–9.</u> Look through these other references to Paul's work in collecting for the poor in Jerusalem to get a bigger view of this long-term important project in his ministry.

PERSONAL STUDY QUESTIONS—LESSON FOUR

Chapter 5

What does Paul mean by "union with Christ"?

What three themes on Christoformity will the next few chapters cover? See the bottom of page 28 in *Reading Romans Backwards*.

Chapter 6

What did you think "spiritual worship" meant before you read this chapter?

List the six points about embodied sacrifice enumerated in the text.

1.
2.
3.
4.
5.
6.

List the six points about prayer.

1.
2.
3.
4.
5.
6.

Chapter 7

When do you find yourself being *superminded*? How does Paul's encouragement toward others-orientation help you change your thinking about other bodies in the Body?

What do the Greek words *soma*, *ekklesia*, and *demos* mean? See the definitions on page 36 of *Reading Romans Backwards*.

Quiz Questions—Lesson Four

1. Two aspects of embodied God-orientation are:
    A. Sacrifice and prayer
    B. Sacrifice and generosity
    C. Prayer and body life
    D. Generosity and goodness

2. Which of these was NOT one of the six points about embodied sacrifice?
    A. God's mercy enables sacrifice
    B. Sacrifice is seen best in generous financial giving
    C. What Christians *do* is the sacrifice
    D. The sacrifice involves transformed minds

3. Which of these was NOT one of the six points about prayer?
    A. Paul's prayers describe attributes of God
    B. Paul's prayers ask God to give other Christians godly traits
    C. Paul asks others to pray for him
    D. Paul prays to the Holy Spirit

True or False

4. Paul tells the Weak and Strong to keep thinking highly of themselves.

5. Paul says the spiritual gifts are for the benefit of the ones who possess them.

LESSON FIVE

BEFORE CLASS

❏ Read Chapter 7, pages 39–43 (5 pages)
❏ Read Romans 12:14–13:10
❏ Read Chapter 8 (6 pages)
❏ Answer the Personal Study Questions

MAIN TAKEAWAY

As the Roman church members became more Christoform, Paul expected them to be at Peace with each other and with their non-Christian Roman neighbors. They should live in the church in unity and tolerance with each other, honoring each other's differences of conscience and welcoming each other at meals. They should live in love toward their neighbors outside the church, being good citizens as shown by paying their taxes and by giving generously toward the public good.

TERMS AND DEFINITIONS

Chapter 8

Benevolence   A feeling or disposition toward kindness and helping others or an act of charity and generosity, giving tangibly to people to need.

CHAPTER SUMMARIES

Chapter 7: Christoformity Is Embodied Body-of-Christ Orientation (12:3-8; 14–15; 16:17-20)

Peace and Unity

- Paul wants the churches as a whole to be at peace with the Roman empire, and Paul wants the individuals in the churches to be at peace with each other.
- "... nearly every verse in 14:1–15:13 is somehow connected to both Weak and Strong learning to live in unity with one another" (39).
- "The condescending judgments of the Strong and the reactive judgments of the Weak in the Roman churches are divisive" (39). The dissention is diabolical, and the way to crush it is through sibling-like welcoming.

Tolerance

- In the kingdom of God lived out on earth, that is, the church, food should no longer divide people.
- Paul affirms both the acceptability of diverse views and the acceptability of having personal conscience limits. They can have different convictions, but they should never push each other to violate their convictions.
- They show love to each other by respecting their differences rather than coercing each other. They show faith by following their own consciences.

Welcoming to the Table

- "Are you the Strong dining with the Weak or not? Yes or no? That's the question, and *the whole book rides on that question as the heart of lived theology*" (41). Welcoming each other at shared meals is how both sides show they are becoming Christoform.
- Paul develops his argument for accepting each other, just as Jesus accepted them, by quoting Old Testament verses about the Gentiles praising and rejoicing.

Chapter 8: Christoformity Is Public Orientation (12:14–13:10)

- As the Christians become more Christ-like, Paul expects this to show in the way they reach outside their churches to love others in public ways.
- Loving neighbors is the first and most important part of a public orientation.

Public Ethics

- The Weak might have struggled more with loving their Roman neighbors than the Strong did because of the harm and prejudice the Jews suffered because of Rome, especially the results of Claudius's expulsion of them.
- Roman taxation was also an issue that may have made the Weak frustrated with the Roman public and therefore not wanting to love outwardly.
- This section of the text runs from 12:14 to 13:10. The instructions about obeying governing authorities are in the middle of a longer discussion about how Christians can show love to non-Christians around them.
- Paul gives four brilliant strategies for loving outsiders: bless them, empathize with them, make peace with them, and love them—even the enemies.
- "One person's subjection is another's oppression" (48).
- A conservative interpretation of this passage on governing authorities is that God acts through authorities, Paul is encouraging the Romans not to revolt, and he might be doing this to protect the small number of Christians from being crushed by the empire.
- Another interpretation is to see Paul calling for some kind of revolution, in keeping with the tradition of Jews opposing foreign powers who pressed them to disobey Torah. Obeying the government had limits when the government asked God's people to disobey God.
- Paul seems to be calling for non-vengeance, for responding to mistreatment with blessing and love. This could add *subjection* as a fifth strategy for loving outsiders.
- Though God orders government, governments sometimes do evil. God is ultimately in control, as King Jesus is over all other powers.
- "Paul knows the way of the cross: the followers of Jesus in Rome are to pay taxes and submit to those dedicated authorities as a way of blessing, peacemaking, and loving one's enemies into neighbors" (49).

Public Benevolence

- Roman gift-giving was not a one-way, altruistic effort. Obligation and reciprocation were expected.
- Offering public benevolence and working/giving toward the common good of neighbors in the Empire seem to be what Paul is encouraging. Paul wants the Weak to give voluntarily rather than rebel against taxation.

This stone in Corinth has the name "Erastus," the city treasurer, likely the person Paul mentions in Romans 16, Acts 19, and 2 Timothy 4. This is an example of public works for good—Erastus likely paid for something important for the city. This is part of the cursus honorum, *receiving public honor for doing public good.*

Group Discussion Questions

Have you ever shared a meal with someone from a very different culture or with a very different diet? Share your experience with the class.

What convictions have you observed in other Christians that have frustrated you? Have you ever tried to convince another believer to change their personal conscience on an issue?

Taxation and public benevolence are the issues Paul has in mind in his discussion of obeying governing authorities. What political issues do Christians deal with today, and how might Paul's words on loving our neighbors outside the church affect how we think about those specific issues?

In Scot McKnight's classroom with our Master's in New Testament cohort, working on creating an ideological map of Romans and a list of issues in the church that might be culturally equivalent to the issues in the Roman churches. Consider trying these activities with your class.

Group Learning Activity Suggestions

Read several scholarly views on Romans 13 that relate the passage to treatment of refugees. The URL to McKnight's blog post on this subject, which also links to other posts on the topic, is in the Resources section below. Also read about a church in the Netherlands that staged a three-month peaceful protest to protect child refugees (URL in the Resources section). Discuss the application of Romans 13 to these and other political issues today.

Ask students to read about Jewish and non-Jewish Roman diets in the first century (two URLs to get them started are in the Resources section). Plan a potluck meal for your class, either for this class period or the next or even outside class time. Ask students to bring kosher and non-kosher foods that might have been found on a table in a Roman house church. Think about setting up the room to enable reclining at a low table to eat Roman style. *Welcome each other* around your table. Considering the political nature of the discussion in this session, perhaps discussing over a meal will remind everyone to love each other in spite of differences of opinion.

RESOURCES FOR FURTHER INFORMATION

- Article about Jewish food from around the world in history and today, with pictures
  http://bit.ly/JewishFood101
- Article about the diet of Romans in the first century
  http://bit.ly/RomanFood101
- More about the expulsion of the Jewish believers from Rome under Claudius
  http://bit.ly/ClaudiusExpulsion
- McKnight's blog post looking at how to interpret and apply Romans 13 in a recent American political discussion. See also the excellent posts he links to from that post by Michael Gorman, Tim Gombis, and Michael Bird.
  http://bit.ly/JesusCreedRom13
- Read about how a Dutch church peacefully but boldly resisted government action, saving child refugees from deportation to dangerous areas, by holding continuous church services for three months.
  http://bit.ly/DutchRefugee
- More on taxes and public benevolence in the Roman Empire
  http://bit.ly/RomanTaxes
- Roman coins and images
  http://bit.ly/RomanCoins

FURTHER BIBLE STUDY

❑ Read the Old Testament quotations in Romans 15 in their contexts: Psalm 18:49 (read verses 46-50), Deuteronomy 32:43 (read 31:30 and 32:39-47), Psalm 117:1 (read both verses, 1 and 2), Isaiah 11:10 (read verses 1-3 and 10-12). Then read Romans 15:7-13.

PERSONAL STUDY QUESTIONS—LESSON FIVE

Chapter 7

Look up the verses in which Paul tells the Roman Christians to welcome each other and summarize or copy them here (Romans 14:1, 14:3, and 15:7).

How does McKnight define "kingdom of God" in the middle of page 40?

What are the five guidelines on tolerance on pages 40–41?

   1.
   2.
   3.
   4.
   5.

What are the four moves toward welcome on page 42?

   1.
   2.
   3.
   4.

Chapter 8

What is the outline McKnight gives of this section of the biblical text? See page 47.

What are four strategies Paul gives for loving those outside the church, in the public, on page 47?

   1.
   2.
   3.
   4.

What is the fifth he adds on page 49?

   5.

Quiz Questions—Lesson Five

1. Which of these is NOT a theme of body-of-Christ orientation?

    A.   Generosity
    B.   Peace and unity
    C.   Civil obedience
    D.   Welcoming to the table

2. What was the first priority when looking at public orientation?

    A.   Love
    B.   Joy
    C.   Peace
    D.   Faith

3. Which of these was a strategy for loving neighbors outside the church?

    A.   Table fellowship
    B.   Communion
    C.   Speaking in tongues
    D.   Empathizing

True or False

4. God's covenant is made first with Israel and then, through them, also with the Gentiles.

5. A public orientation would probably have been harder for the Strong than for the Weak.

LESSON SIX

BEFORE CLASS

- ❑ Read Romans 13:11-14
- ❑ Read Chapter 9 (3 pages)
- ❑ Read Romans 9, 10, and 11
- ❑ Read Chapter 10 (9 pages)
- ❑ Answer the Personal Study Questions

MAIN TAKEAWAY

Chapter 9: In light of what has happened in the past in the story of God's people, what is happening in our age now, and what will happen in the future, we need to live lives of righteousness, putting on the ways of God by putting on Christoformity.

Chapter 10: The whole section of chapters 9–11 is not about individual salvation or predestination. Rather, it is about God's choice of redemptive agents throughout history. God has always intended a corporate salvation, the formation of a community of God's people, and God has made surprising choices along the way about who will play the roles of redemptive work.

TERMS AND DEFINITIONS

Chapter 9

Eschatology	The study of the end of time and the final victory of God.
Imminency and immanency	Imminent means something that will be happening or coming soon. Immanent means present in the universe. Here it is used regarding a new era in history. "The time is at hand" means that the time is immediately arriving and the time is now in existence.

45

Chapter 10

Recapitulation The summarizing of what has been learned so far. Here it means repeating what we've learned about the context of Romans. Used in a theological sense, recapitulation is an atonement theory that God sums up or brings together everything in Jesus (see Ephesians 1:10).

Chapter Summaries

Chapter 9: Know the Time Is Now (13:11-14)

- "The clunker in the conversation is that we differ sometimes so dramatically that we either quarrel with one another or must conclude that each person must make up her or his own mind about each moral decision—which of course is fine until you conclude something that impacts me, which is what was happening in Rome among the house churches" (51)
- Sometimes our ethics or moral judgments come from revelation from God / from above / law. Sometimes they come from wise insight / from below / wisdom. Sometimes they come from the future kingdom / from beyond / prophecy.
- In eschatological ethics, there are two points: first, looking at the time and, second, seeing how to live.
- A Christian view of time can be broken into four timeframes. First was original creation and the fall and God's covenant. Second was Jesus's coming and redeeming the world and then sending the Spirit to the church (we live in this time now). Third will be the battle against and defeat of evil. Fourth will be the future kingdom reign of God. God's rule is both now and not yet.
- The Christians in Rome are supposed to examine how they live in this second epoch and make sure they are taking off the old clothes / ways of the world and putting on the new clothes / ways of the kingdom. Their infighting is as much a way of the world as the notorious debauched sins are ways of the world.
- The new clothes the Roman Christians are called to put on are Christ himself—this is what it means to be Christoformed.

Chapter 10: Where We've Been, Where We Are, Where We're Headed
(9-11)

- Romans is often taught as theoretical theology instead of lived theology because many commentators do not take into consideration the context for Romans. "Romans is a pastoral theology front to back or, in our case, back to front, and its deepest concern is Peace, not Privilege, not Power" (57)
- Review of the context of Romans: Phoebe represented Paul as she delivered and read the letter to the Roman house churches. They were located in poor areas of Rome, and they were made up of both Jewish (Weak) and Gentile (Strong) followers of Jesus. The Jewish believers had been kicked out of Rome and were now coming back, finding the churches changed to being primarily Gentile and no longer being focused on practicing Torah. They found a heavy burden of taxation as well. The Weak observe Torah and look down on the Strong for not doing the same. The Strong, and Paul is among them, have higher social status in the culture, and they criticize the Weak for their convictions and practice. Paul is seeking to blend both groups into the family of God, to bring Peace into the conflict in the churches, and he teaches Peace by way of Christoformity for both Weak and Strong.
- The Strong (Gentiles) knew the stories and laws of Rome. The Weak (Jews) knew the stories of Israel and the laws of Moses. For them all to come together as the covenant people of God, they needed to learn the same story. For the Strong, this meant learning the story of Israel. For the Weak, this meant relearning their own story as it becomes the story of the unified church.
- "The story Paul tells is the symbolic universe he wants the Strong and the Weak to inhabit together. Reading Romans backwards stands alongside Paul's reading of Israel's history backwards—that is, reading Israel's history in light of what happens to the people of God in Christ" (59).
- Paul tells the stories of major characters, women and men, in Israel's narrative. Their inclusion in his story is not about their personal salvation but about God's choosing them to play important roles in the history.
- Paul tells the story of Israel to fit his mission in bringing Peace between Strong and Weak in Rome. He retells it in the tradition of other Jewish storytellers who also reconfigure the narrative to fit their needs. Similar retellings can be found in Deuteronomy 28–30, Sirach 44–51, 1 Maccabees 2:51-64, Acts 7, and Hebrews 11.

- Paul lists many events in the history, not in chronological order, all driving toward a point: "The theme is not how to get saved, or even who is saved, but God's covenant faithfulness. Paul reconfigures Israel's story to form a narrative about God's surprising faithfulness in the missionary movement to include Gentiles into the one family of God, Israel. That inclusive narrative promotes peace among the Strong and the Weak." (page 61)
- Paul makes many references to a range of Old Testament texts in building his argument. This seems clearly targeted at the Weak in the audiences as Phoebe read. This view on the intended audience of 9:1–11:12 is reinforced by Paul's statement in 11:13 that he is beginning to address the Gentiles (Strong), meaning he was not addressing them in the previous verses.
- One of Paul's major rhetorical strategies is asking questions. Most of his questions in this section seem aimed at the arguments of the Weak about their Privilege in being the covenant owners.
- "He creates a narrative of Israel's history that establishes Israel's election as well as God's surprising moves, and he creates this narrative so he can include the Messiah, who includes Gentiles in God's plan" (64).
- In response to the deeply felt question of the Weak about whether they were still God's covenant chosen ones, and whether God would be faithful to the covenant, Paul is answering Yes! "God is faithful because God continues to work through Israel for the world's redemption" (64).

Group Discussion Questions

Ask several students to tell their own life stories briefly, structuring their stories to highlight the surprising twists and choices God has brought into their life, which they can see clearly now looking backwards.

What various opinions on predestination for personal salvation do the students hold? Share and discuss.

How many have been taught personal salvation as the theme of Romans?

Group Learning Activity Suggestions

Work together as a class to put the people and the events of Israel's story, as mentioned in Romans 9 through 11, in chronological order—how they happened in the Old Testament, as opposed to the order Paul puts them in.

Build a visual family tree of the matriarchs and patriarchs. Ask students to choose their characters from the list you created. Considering bringing in props or costumes to the class. Set up tables and chairs of several heights (keeping safety in mind!) and stage a living picture that shows the descendants in the family line and highlights God's surprising choices. Make sure to take pictures!

Look up the texts mentioned on page 60 of *Reading Romans Backwards*: Deuteronomy 28–30, Sirach 44–51, 1 Maccabees 2:51-64, Acts 7, and Hebrews 11. (URLs to Sirach and 1 Maccabees are in the Resources section.) Divide the students into groups with each group working on one text and comparing it to Romans 9–11. After the groups finish, ask each group to present the similarities and differences they found to the class.

Ask a student to read Paul's questions out loud in the style of an aggressive prosecuting attorney. After they are finished, ask the rest of the class what effect it had on them. How do they feel? How might the Weak in the house churches have felt as Phoebe presented Paul's questions? (See page 63 in *Reading Romans Backwards* for the questions.)

RESOURCES FOR FURTHER INFORMATION

- Article arguing why Romans 9 is about individual election. This is counter to McKnight's view and may provide information for an interesting class discussion.
  http://bit.ly/IndividualElection
- Read Sirach online
  http://bit.ly/SirachOnline
- Read 1 Maccabees online
  http://bit.ly/1MaccabeesOnline

FURTHER BIBLE STUDY

❑ Isaiah 40:13 and Job 41:11. Read these verses in the context of the verses around them then look at how Paul uses them in Romans 11:34-35.

PERSONAL STUDY QUESTIONS—LESSON SIX

Chapter 9

Write a paragraph, in your own words, explaining the context of Romans to someone who is about to begin reading the epistle.

What are the four timeframes in the Christian view of time?
1.
2.
3.
4.

How can you put on the new clothes of Christoformity in your life?

Chapter 10

Scan through Romans 9–11, and write down all the people Paul names.

Scan through Romans 9–11, and write down all the Scripture references Paul uses.

Put into your own words the theme of the story Paul tells about Israel.

Quiz Questions—Lesson Six

1. How many questions does Paul batter the Weak with?

    A. 20
    B. 21
    C. 15
    D. 12

2. What five topics does this lesson look at in Romans 9–11?

    A. Predestination, Calvinism, Arminianism, salvation, election
    B. Persons, narrative comparisons, events, texts, questions
    C. Context, history, Old Testament texts, prophets, Israel
    D. Patriarchs, narrative comparisons, events, citations, exodus

3. Romans 9–11 answers this question:

    A. Who are the gospel agents in God's redemptive plan?
    B. Who gets saved?
    C. Why is God unfaithful?
    D. What is the reason that Gentiles should observe the Torah?

True or False

4. The question of the Weak is: "Is not Israel the elect people of God?"

5. The question of the Strong is: "Is it not the case that God has moved from Israel to the Gentiles in salvation through the cosmic Lord Jesus?"

LESSON SEVEN

CHAPTER 11

Before class

- ☐ Read Romans 9:1 through 11:10
- ☐ Read Chapter 11 (14 pages)
- ☐ Answer the Personal Study Questions

Main takeaway

The Weak—the Torah-observant Jewish believers in Rome—are wondering how to make sense of God's covenant promises when they see many Jews not following Jesus as Messiah but see many Gentiles following Jesus instead. Paul wants them to understand that they are God's chosen / elect people, and also the election now extends to the Gentiles through Jesus.

Terms and Definitions

Election   God's choice of people for God's purposes. Sometimes it is used to mean those individuals God has chosen to be saved, sometimes it means God's choice of a people group to be God's people, and sometimes it means God's choice of people to use for certain roles or designs.

Chapter Summaries

Chapter 11: To the Weak (9:1–11:10)

- Six transformational themes in Romans 9–11 are:
    1. mercy and wrath
    2. Gentiles and remnant
    3. righteousness rooted in law or faith
    4. divinely chosen remnant as well as the hardened
    5. the failure of both Jews and Gentiles

6. the correlations of Israel's hardening and Gentile inclusion along with Gentile fullness and Israel's eschatological redemption

- Paul is speaking to the Jewish believers, specifically the Weak, in this section (9:1–11:10). This conclusion is substantiated by the many Hebrew Scripture references and the focus of the questions that seem targeted at that audience. In 11:13, Paul turns to begin addressing the Gentiles, the Strong.
- The Israelites have the Privilege of being God's elect people.
- The "covenants" may mean just the covenant with Abraham but likely also include the Mosaic and Davidic covenants as well as the new covenant in Jesus, as prophesied in Jeremiah.
- Part of their Privilege is the honor of knowing their patriarchs and matriarchs are the physical ancestors of their Messiah.
- Paul highlights the surprise of God's choices in election. God has always surprised the people with God's choices of who will play the next part in the redemptive history. It is in keeping with God's plan and intention all along to also elect Gentiles to join the covenant people. This means the elective Privilege is no longer exclusive but is now shared.
- McKnight assumes the Weak are asking this question: "How can Israel, which has been God's people and has been striving for the kingdom of God all along, be excluded while Gentiles, who truth be told have lived in sin all along, are the ones upon whom God's favor now rests?" (70)
- The answer to that question is this: "The Messiah (9:30–10:4) proves both God's faithfulness to the covenant and expands that covenant to include the Gentiles (the Strong in Rome) without diminishing the election of Israel (the Weak)" (71).
- The way of Peace between Strong and Weak is settling the issue of Torah observance. Peace comes "not by way of imposing Torah but by allegiance to King Jesus and to life in the Spirit" for both Jew and Gentile (72).
- The three- in-one problem is "(1) Israel, works, Torah as boundary markers; (2) faith and Messiah; and (3) Gentiles and faith" (72).
- Works of the law here mean observing food laws, keeping Sabbath, and maintaining circumcision.
- Paul is trying to show them that righteousness comes through faith, and now that Jesus has been the perfectly faithful Israelite, righteousness comes through faith in him. The believing Gentiles have achieved righteousness through allegiance to Jesus, while some Jews have

not achieved righteousness—because of the twin issues of trying to achieve it by works of the law and by rejecting the righteous Messiah.

- Paul's argument is not against Judaism; it's against the Weak thinking the Strong need to observe Torah. Paul shows that God has always acted in surprising grace, not individual merit, not status gained from Torah observance, so that doesn't need to start now with the Gentile believers.

- Paul quotes Leviticus 18 and Deuteronomy 30 and reinterprets them to be about the new covenant, now revealed in Jesus. Those who are circumcised in their hearts (allegiant to Jesus) are made righteous in the new covenant. This shows the difference between those who see Jesus as the stumbling block and those who see him as the Messiah.

- Romans 10:13 changes the topic to mission. Just as the Jews were called to bless all nations, now that some from the nations (the Gentiles) have been brought into the people of God by faith, they have the same calling: to bless all the nations with the Good News about Jesus the Messiah.

- "Paul embodies God's faithfulness to Israel. . . . Paul sees himself as an example of Jewish belief in the Messiah, a challenge to fellow Jews to join him in the Messiah, and a model to imitate when it comes to fellowship with the Strong and the Weak" (78). Elijah is also an embodiment, perhaps of those who plead with God.

- "Paul's words shaped for the Weak in Rome are all designed as both comfort and warning: comfort to know they are the elect, the remnant, recipients of grace, and those who know the faithfulness of God to his covenant with Israel. The warning is that they are to believe and remain faithful, for God's ways are surprisingly sovereign" (80).

- Three important terms sum up the message to the Weak. God *elected* Israelites with surprising *grace*, not based on human merit. The faithful who believe in Jesus are the *remnant*.

GROUP DISCUSSION QUESTIONS

What, if anything, had you previously learned or believed about election? (Some Christian traditions focus much more on this topic than others.)

Look at Romans 10:13-15 and the outline of that section on page 76. Trace the path for mission, going backwards from *sent* and ending at *call*. Create a diagram together of Paul's concept of mission.

Work together to summarize Paul's answer to the question of the Weak: Is God faithful to us?

GROUP LEARNING ACTIVITY SUGGESTIONS

Divide the class in half. One side will be the Weak and the other side will be the Strong. Let the Weak try to convince the Strong to observe Torah and let the Strong argue back.

Ask a student to read 1 Kings 19:1-18 out loud, slowly and dramatically, to the class. Then work together to make a list of all the similarities between Elijah and Paul and between the ideas in 1 King 19 and Romans 9–11.

RESOURCES FOR FURTHER INFORMATION

- Calvinism versus Arminianism often comes up in discussions on election. Here is information comparing and contrasting the two perspectives.
  http://bit.ly/CalvinismVersusArminianism
- How Jews practice Shabbat (Sabbath) today
  http://bit.ly/ShabbatToday

FURTHER BIBLE STUDY

- ❑ Isaiah 1:9 and 10:22-23. Look at these verses in context to see what they say about the remnant.
- ❑ Deuteronomy 29:4, Isaiah 29:10, Psalm 69:22-23. Read these verses in their contexts, then look again at how Paul uses them in Romans 11:7-10.

Personal Study Questions—Lesson Seven

When have you felt sorrow or grief over the spiritual struggles of people you care about? Describe the situation. (See Paul's grief in 9:1-3 and 10:1-3)

What is the way to achieve Peace between the Strong and the Weak? (see page 72)

Who are the three characters in the conversation as imagined by Matthew Bates? (See page 75). How does this approach help make sense of the issues in Romans 9–11?

How does Jesus as Messiah reshape the Weak's understanding of Israel's election?

Quiz Questions—Lesson Seven

1. Which one is NOT one of the three characters in Matthew Bates's perspective on 10:5-13?

    A.   Paul
    B.   Righteousness by Faith
    C.   A presumptuous person
    D.   The Judge

2. What do "works of the law" mean in Romans 9–11?

    A.   Observing food laws, keeping Sabbath, practicing circumcision
    B.   Any sort of good deeds that attempt to earn salvation
    C.   The 10 Commandments
    D.   The law of Moses

3. Which is NOT one of the three key terms in this lesson?

    A.   Election
    B.   Grace
    C.   Welcome
    D.   Remnant

True or False

4. The three-in-one problem is (1) Israel, works, Torah as boundary markers; (2) faith and Messiah; and (3) election privilege.

5. The Messiah is the stumbling stone.

LESSON EIGHT

Before class

- ❏ Read Romans 11:1-36
- ❏ Read Chapter 12 (8 pages)
- ❏ Answer the Personal Study Questions

Main takeaway

The Strong are grafted onto the rootstock of God's covenant while the unbelieving Jews are torn off. Paul warns the Strong that the way they are acting in pride toward the Weak is not Christlike, and disobedience like that could get them torn off as well. Israel seeing the Gentiles grafted in will cause them jealousy or zeal, and eventually they will be grafted back in themselves.

Terms and Definitions

Correlation	A dependent relationship or connection between two variables
A fortiori	A type of logical argument that draws a second conclusion from a first, already proven, conclusion

Chapter Summaries

Chapter 12: To the Strong (11:1-36)

- There are five integrated themes in this chapter: jealousy, correlation, expansion and warning, temporary unbelief, and Israel's redemptive future
- Paul thinks that the faith of the Gentiles, and God's acceptance of them, will create jealousy/zeal in the Israelites, ultimately leading them to faith in Jesus. His logic goes like this: "Israel rejects Jesus as Messiah and so stumbles over him; Israel's stumbling prompts Gentile

belief in Jesus; Gentile faith provokes the zeal of Israelites; this zeal/ jealousy prompts Israelites to repent and turn in faith in Jesus as Messiah; and finally God's faithfulness to the covenant with Israel is established" (82).

- The inclusion of the Strong correlates to Israel's rejection of Jesus. The Israelite stumbling led to the Gentile inclusion, and the Gentile inclusion will eventually lead to the Israelite acceptance of Jesus.

- God's covenant grace is the root, and Israel is the branches. Israel's stubborn unbelief in the Messiah led to their being broken off the rootstock, making room for the Gentiles to be grafted in. The Jews and Gentiles share the nourishment from the roots of covenant.

- The Strong are acting in arrogance toward the Weak, using their Privilege and Power to coerce. Paul warns them that acting in unbelief like this, instead of continuing in faith, could get them broken off, just like unbelieving Israel is broken off. They need to use their Power to serve and embrace the Weak as siblings, leading to Peace.

- Israel's unbelief is temporary. Once the Gentiles have come in to the family, "all Israel" will believe and be saved. This is because of God's faithfulness, because God's gift (the covenant root of grace) is irrevocable.

- What does "all Israel" mean here? It could be ethnic Israel/Israel in the flesh/Abraham's actual descendants. It could be Israel in the flesh PLUS Israel by faith. It could be Israel expanded (Jewish believers and Gentile believers). It could be Israel as a symbol of the church. McKnight argues that "all Israel" means Israel-in-the-flesh and Israel-by-faith-in-the-Messiah, together with Gentile believers.

GROUP DISCUSSION QUESTIONS

Paul says that the "gifts and calling" of Israel's God "are irrevocable" (11:29). McKnight says this means the root of the tree, the covenant grace of God. How have you heard this taught before in church or Bible study?

Do you know any Christians acting like the "Strong" toward others today? If Paul were to confront them, what might he say to them to correct their behavior?

What do you think about Paul's idea that the Gentile inclusion will provoke jealousy and ultimately belief among the Jews?

GROUP LEARNING ACTIVITY SUGGESTIONS

Read John 15:1-17 out loud to the class. Then go through the verses together, side by side with Romans 11:13-24. Make a list of the similarities and differences between Jesus's analogy and Paul's. Do you think Paul had heard this teaching of Jesus and had it in mind when he wrote his analogy?

Watch the video of grafting vines (URL in Resources) and discuss.

Look in the Resources section for URLs to three articles that interpret 11:29 to mean that the "gifts and callings" are the spiritual gifts and ministry callings God gives to individuals. The interpretation is that only God can give these to people, and only God can take them away. What was the result of that interpretation in these situations?

RESOURCES FOR FURTHER INFORMATION

- Short video of grafting onto rootstock
  http://bit.ly/GraftingVines
- Articles interpreting Romans 11:29 as being about personal ministry gifts and calls
  http://bit.ly/HaginGifts
  http://bit.ly/MartinGifts
  http://bit.ly/WaitsGifts
  http://bit.ly/HaggardGifts
- Discussion by Pete Enns about Paul's use of Old Testament quotations, primarily in Romans 9–11
  http://bit.ly/PaulEvangelical

FURTHER BIBLE STUDY

❑ Acts 5:17, 13:45, and 17:5. Examples of Jewish leaders acting in jealousy/zeal.

❑ Exodus 20:5, Deuteronomy 32:16, Joshua 24:19. References to God as jealous.

Personal Study Questions—Lesson Eight

What is the difference between jealousy and envy in English?

How might you define biblical jealousy?

What analogies or images of correlation does Paul use? (See page 83.) Draw pictures to illustrate the analogies.

What do the Strong need to do differently in the way they see and treat the Weak?

What does "all Israel" mean in this section when talking about "all Israel will be saved"?

QUIZ QUESTIONS—LESSON EIGHT

1. Which of these is NOT one of the five themes in this lesson?

    A. Jealousy
    B. Temporary unbelief
    C. Expansion and warning
    D. Circumcision

2. Which object is part of an analogy Paul makes about the correlation of the Strong?

    A. Sheep
    B. Stars
    C. Dough
    D. Thread

3. God is jealous when the people are:

    A. Idolaters
    B. Disobedient
    C. Unfaithful
    D. All of the above

True or False

4. The Strong could lose their place on the rootstock by their disobedience.

5. All Israel will be saved.

LESSON NINE

CHAPTER 13, CHAPTER 14

BEFORE CLASS

❑ Read Romans 1:1-17
❑ Read Chapter 13 (9 pages)
❑ Read Romans 1 and 2
❑ Read Chapter 14 (6 pages)
❑ Answer the Personal Study Questions

MAIN TAKEAWAY

Paul's gospel is more than a message of individual salvation. His gospel is the story of Jesus the Messiah, the story of the Hebrew Scriptures and the Jewish Messiah, who plans to bless and include all the people of the nations who will be allegiant and obedient to him through faith. In the beginning of Romans, Paul is talking to Jews about moral transformation. He says it does not come through Torah observance but through Christoformity.

TERMS AND DEFINITIONS

Chapter 13

Semitism	A word, phrase, or idiom from a Semitic language such as Hebrew.
Ambit	The scope or range or bounds of something, here used for the boundaries of the power of God for redemption.

Chapter 14

Soteriology	The study of the beliefs, theology, and doctrine of salvation.
Diatribe	An angry verbal rant.

CHAPTER SUMMARIES

Chapter 13: The Opening to the Letter (1:1-17)

- Romans 1–4 and 5–8 could be considered separate sections, but they work together.
- Reviewing the previous chapters, we are reminded that we must keep in mind the lived theology and context of the letter as we begin chapters 1–8. We're looking for Christoformity leading to peace between the Weak and the Strong.
- Paul introduces himself as an apostle and a slave, which leads into his introducing his mission to the Gentiles and talking about the gospel.
- Paul's gospel is the story of Jesus the Messiah, and it's a very Jewish story from the Hebrew Scriptures. It is Israel's story, which is the story of the Weak, and the Strong are grafted into it. Paul expands the gospel to include the Gentile mission.
- The term "Messiah" could be for the Weak and "Lord" for the Strong—ways to view Jesus that relate to their different cultures.
- ". . . for Paul grace creates faith and faith creates obedience" (95), but disobedience in the unloving way they are treating each other is an issue of both Strong and Weak. Obedience of faith is another way of looking at Christoformity.
- Paul's thanksgiving is personal and affectionate, missional, gospel-oriented (not to convert them but to transform them), and not-ashamed which turns upside down Romans ideas of status.
- Paul's four glorious themes about the gospel are: 1. the gospel saves, meaning that God-in-Christ does a work of new creation in us; 2. gospel faith is allegiance; 3. the gospel saves first Jews and second Gentiles; and 4. the gospel shows God's righteousness and faithfulness.
- The phrase "Through faith for faith" is unclear and has much scholarly debate around it. McKnight's suggestion is: "perhaps he means the Strong's faith ('through faith') and the Weak's need 'for faith,' just as we can read it vice versa." Or, "fulfillment of the Abrahamic promise of Genesis 12:3. Thus, 'from faith' points back to Abraham, and 'unto faith' to the fulfillment in the church" (99).

Chapter 14: The Rhetoric of Romans 1–2

- Who is being addressed in this section of text? A traditional way of reading this section "is that he presents bad news (1:18–3:20), the good news (3:21-26), and how to get it (3:27–4:25). This standard reading has a clear agenda: it *universalizes the soteriology of Paul.* It also removes the message from the social context sketched in Romans 12–16" (101).

- Romans 1:18-32 does not seem to be about all humans or all Gentiles but rather is about a Jewish stereotype of Gentile sinfulness, of a pagan idol worshipper. This sounds similar to Wisdom of Solomon, which also connected idolatry with wild sins. It seems to be talking *about* Gentiles *to* Jews.
- Disobedience to God results in God's allowing the people to sin, handing them over to the results of their choices.
- Romans 2:1-2 shifts the rhetoric. The Judge, who is likely representative of the Weak's point of view, is judging the Gentile sinners in chapter 1, and then Paul turns on the Judge and points out, "You . . . are doing the very same things" (105).
- The term for judge is found again in chapter 14 in the view of the Weak toward the Strong. The Judge seems to be those of the Weak who judge the Strong as idolaters who don't observe Torah.
- "Romans 1–8 occur then in two blocks: the argument against Torah observance as the path to moral transformation, and an argument in favor of union with Christ and Spirit-indwelling as the true path to moral transformation" (106).

The synagogue in Sardis could have held 1,000 people. It's located right in the heart of the city. It might have been converted from a Greco-Roman building to a synagogue and seems to have maintained some Roman symbolism including the eagles and lions. The large stone table would have been used for rolling out the Torah scrolls to read. Paul did some of his missionary work in synagogues like these.

GROUP DISCUSSION QUESTIONS

Review the context for Romans together. What is Paul's goal in teaching lived theology to the house churches of Rome?

How would you write a stereotyped description of notorious sinners today?

Do you think God's handing people over to sin and consequences has anything to do with God's hardening of Pharaoh? Are they the same thing or not? Related? Why or why not?

GROUP LEARNING ACTIVITY SUGGESTIONS

Read through the openings of some of Paul's letters in roughly chronological order: 1 Thessalonians 1:1-6, Galatians 1:1-6, 1 Corinthians 1:1-9, Philippians 1:1-8, Philemon 1–7, and 2 Corinthians 1:1-5. What do you notice about how he identifies himself, greets them, and talks about God?

Ask each student to write the opening of a letter to their church or small group or a collection of friends. Instructions: Greet them, introduce yourself, and lead into the theological topic you want to share with them, all in the style of Paul.

Watch the Seven Minute Seminary video of McKnight talking about the gospel (URL in Resources). Does this differ from how you have thought of the gospel before? If so, how? How does this help your understanding of the discussion of the gospel in this lesson?

RESOURCES FOR FURTHER INFORMATION

- Seven Minute Seminary video on Scot McKnight on what is the gospel
  http://bit.ly/SMcKGospel
- To read even more about McKnight's views on the biblical gospel, read his book *The King Jesus Gospel*.

FURTHER BIBLE STUDY

❑ Romans 1:3-4, 1 Timothy 2:8, and 1 Corinthians 15:1-8. Study what Paul means by "gospel."

PERSONAL STUDY QUESTIONS—LESSON NINE

Chapter 13

Summarize the previous section of *Reading Romans Backwards*, about chapters 9–11, in your own words.

How does Paul describe himself in the opening of Romans?

What is Paul's mission?

What are the four gospel themes on pages 97–98?

1.
2.
3.
4.

Chapter 14

What people are described in 1:18-32?

Who is the judge?

What are the two blocks into which Romans 1–8 can be divided?

QUIZ QUESTIONS—LESSON NINE

1. Which one is NOT one of the four gospel themes in this lesson?

   A. The gospel saves
   B. Gospel faith is allegiance
   C. The gospel saves first Gentiles and second Jews
   D. The gospel shows God's righteousness and faithfulness

2. The prophet Paul quotes who contrasts the proud with the righteous who live by faith is:

   A. Habakkuk
   B. Isaiah
   C. Hosea
   D. Micah

3. Paul is not ashamed of

   A. His stance as the Strong
   B. Being a slave of Christ
   C. The gospel
   D. His Roman citizenship

True or False

4. The term "Messiah" could appeal to the Strong and "Lord" to the Weak.

5. The phrase "Through faith for faith" is clear and has been consistently interpreted.

LESSON TEN

BEFORE CLASS

- ❏ Read Romans 2
- ❏ Read Chapter 15 (7 pages)
- ❏ Read Romans 3:1-26
- ❏ Read Chapter 16 (10 pages)
- ❏ Answer the Personal Study Questions

MAIN TAKEAWAY

Paul addresses "the Judge," a character who stands among the Weak in Rome. This Judge is looking down on notorious Gentile sinners, but the Judge is a hypocrite who also sins. God's judgment is not based on Torah observance but on obeying God by the power of the Spirit. People are saved by grace but judged by deeds.

The Jewish believers are asking if there is an advantage to being Jewish. Paul says yes, they are advantaged because God gave them the Torah. However, Gentiles can also obey God's revelation, and both Jews and Gentiles sin.

TERMS AND DEFINITIONS

Chapter 16

Covenantal nomism	This is the belief that first-century Judaism is not about trying to earn God's favor through doing good works and following the law (merit theology or works righteousness). Rather it is about God giving the covenant and the people responding to relationship with God by obeying God in order to stay part of the covenant people. God provides atonement for sins in this covenant relationship. E.P. Sanders was a key proponent of this perspective in the 1970s, and this is one of the views of the New Perspective on Paul.

Chapter Summaries

Chapter 15: Reading Romans 2 After Romans 1

- The Weak who judge the Strong will also be judged by God.
- "The audience of Romans 2:17-29 is almost certainly Jewish believers in Jesus" (107). While the audience of the first part of that chapter is up for debate, McKnight believes the audience in 2:1-16 is the same as 2:17-29.
- Reading Romans backwards helps us map the Weak and Strong discussion near the end of the epistle onto the opening chapters, making sense of the rhetoric in 1–4. "The Jew of 2:17 is the Judge of 2:1, and the Judge of 2:1 is the Weak of Romans 14" (108). They are Weak because of the way they judge and look down on the Gentile believers' freedom from Torah.
- Sometimes in Romans interpretation, the limited statements about the Weak (Jewish believers) / the Judge have been taken to be universal statements about all Jews.
- The first rhetorical turnabout is to call the Judge a hypocrite—the Judge does the same sins as those he judges. The second rhetorical turnabout is that God's judgment will not be based on Torah observance but on doing God's will, which the Strong can do as well as the Weak. The third rhetorical turnabout is changing circumcision from a state of the flesh to a state of the heart, a spiritual status of obedience to God's will.
- God's judgment has come to be seen in Christianity as being about personal salvation or punishment. But a more biblical view is that judgment is about God's Peace and justice. Paul's view is that redemption comes by grace, but people are judged by their works.
- God is impartial regarding election and Torah observance—rather, God judges on deeds.
- Torah observance is fine but not required.

Chapter 16: The First Question—Advantage (3:1-26)

- Paul frames Romans 2–4 in a series of questions and answers, addressing the Roman Weak.
- In the next chapters of *Reading Romans Backwards*, McKnight explores three breathtaking questions, possibly familiar to Paul

because Jewish believers asked him those same question on his church planting adventures.

> + Jewish privilege and election—3:1-20
> + Boasting—3:27-31
> + Abraham—4:1-25

- Is there an advantage to being Jewish? "Here is the framework of his answer: 'Yes, the people of Israel have an advantage, but, no, the advantage is not always what is thought'" (116). Paul gives three answers about the Jewish advantage.
- The first answer is the advantage of the Torah, God's revelation. God gave this to the Jews, so they are advantaged.
- The second answer is that the Strong, too, can also obey God's revelation, and it's the obedience that matters.
- The third answer is that the Weak are not actually better off than the Strong because all, both Jews and Gentiles, are slaves to Sin. Torah observance doesn't save anyone from Sin.
- Paul quotes from the Psalms about sinfulness to show the Weak that they are also universally sinful. The Judge sins just like the ones he judges, and since the Judge is the face of the Weak, the Weak need to remember that they sin just like the Strong they are judging.
- Paul identifies with the Jewish believers in his language, such as saying "our," "we," and "all of us."
- What does "works of the law" mean? It "describes the faithful Jew's consistent observance of the Torah . . . on singular and identity-shaping laws like Sabbath, food laws, and circumcision . . . 'works of the law' is far closer to boundary-marking behaviors than to merit-seeking universal human attempts to prove oneself good or honorable enough to survive God's scrutiny" (120).
- The discussion here is over a problem between different groups of Christians, not a problem between Jews and Christians.
- "God's righteousness is both an attribute of God (God is righteous) and a gift of God. It is God's gracious redemptive power at work to make the world right through forgiving sin and establishing righteousness for all" (121–2).
- "God's saving righteousness is not from the Torah, but it is witnessed or testified to by the Torah and the Prophets . . . Their elective privilege remains, but they must not think it comes by way of Torah observance" (122).

- "Justification—the courtroom scene of God's recreating some-one in the right through Christ—is a gift for 'all who have sinned' (3:24)" (123).
- God is faithful and shows that faithfulness through the faithfulness of Jesus.

GROUP DISCUSSION QUESTIONS

What previous knowledge, if any, did you have of first-century Judaism?

Had you ever heard that Judaism is a "works righteousness" religion? How does merit theology / works righteousness contrast with covenantal nomism? In the Resources section, there is a URL to a blog post by McKnight in which he briefly defines covenantal nomism and discusses the New Perspective on Paul.

How would you answer the question, "Is there an advantage to being Jewish?"

GROUP LEARNING ACTIVITY SUGGESTIONS

Assign students to read about various atonement theories before class. Ask them to present briefly on their assigned theory. Adjust the time of their planned presentation according to how many students you have and how long your class period will be. (Two resources to get them started are listed in the Resources section.)

After the presentations, discuss as a class the different views on atonement. Then relate the theories to Romans—how does the your learning so far in this class affect your view of these atonement theories?

Consider watching the short Bible Project video on Atonement and Sacrifice together. URL in Resources.

RESOURCES FOR FURTHER INFORMATION

- McKnight on covenantal nomism and the New Perspective on Paul
  http://bit.ly/McKnightCovenantalNomism
- On page 111, McKnight says, "Somebody quote Dietrich Bonhoeffer!" in the discussion on grace and works. Here are some quotes by Bonhoeffer on grace.
  http://bit.ly/DietrichGrace
- Atonement Theory summaries
  http://bit.ly/AtonementPrimer
  http://bit.ly/TheopediaAtonement

- Pastor Brian Zahnd on understanding the death of Jesus
  http://bit.ly/ZahndAtonement
- Bible Project video on Atonement and Sacrifice
  http://bit.ly/BibleProjectAtonement
- Short video by Old Testament scholar John Walton on "covenant"
  http://bit.ly/WaltonCovenant

FURTHER BIBLE STUDY

❑ Galatians 5:6 and 1 Corinthians 7:19. Read Paul's logic on circumcision in other letters and compare with what he says in Romans.

PERSONAL STUDY QUESTIONS—LESSON TEN

Chapter 15

Describe the Judge (see page 109).

What are the three rhetorical turnabouts?

1.
2.
3.

Chapter 16

What question are the Jewish believers asking?

What are Paul's three answers to that question?

1.
2.
3.

What does "works of the law" mean in these passages?

How does Paul believe that people are transformed?

Quiz Questions—Lesson Ten

1. Which is NOT a descriptor of the Judge?

    A. Relies on the Torah
    B. Is a guide to the blind
    C. Does not know the Torah
    D. Is a corrector of the foolish

2. Which IS one of the three rhetorical turnabouts?

    A. The Judge is a hypocrite
    B. Goats to the right
    C. Torah observance is demanded for the Strong
    D. Circumcision of the flesh is what matters

3. The second of the three principal question is about

    A. Abraham
    B. Advantage
    C. Boasting
    D. Circumcision

True or False

4. The limited statements about the Weak / the Judge have been taken to be universal statements about all Jews.

5. We are saved by faith and judged by works.

LESSON ELEVEN

CHAPTER 17, CHAPTER 18

BEFORE CLASS

- ❑ Read Romans 3:27-31
- ❑ Read Chapter 17 (5 pages)
- ❑ Read Romans 4:1-25
- ❑ Read Chapter 18 (7 pages)
- ❑ Answer the Personal Study Questions

MAIN TAKEAWAY

The Jewish believers think there is an advantage in being Jewish (election privilege and Torah observance), and they boast in this status in the same way that Romans were expected to boast in their accomplishments to advance up the *cursus honorum*. Paul says it's not Torah observance but faith by the Spirit that matters. Abraham is an example: Paul says Abraham was made righteous by faith, not by circumcision or sacrifices. The Strong can also live by faith, which means they are also advantaged in the same way as the Weak.

TERMS AND DEFINITIONS

Chapter 18

Aqedah	The story in Genesis 22 about Abraham being willing to sacrifice his promised son, Isaac. The name comes from the Hebrew word for "binding"—The Binding of Isaac.
Midrash	This can refer to either a genre or a method of Hebrew Bible interpretation. It can be a collection of early Jewish interpretive writings or an approach to interpreting Scripture that often involves creativity and imagination.
Incongruous	Regarding God's grace, incongruous means it's given to those who don't deserve it or haven't earned it.

CHAPTER SUMMARIES

Chapter 17: The Second Question—Boasting in Advantage (3:27-31)

- The Advantage Question now has the addition of Boasting.
- This type of boasting is not the concept of early Christian theologians regarding humans claiming to be worthy of salvation because of their right actions. This is a Greco-Roman concept rooted in the *cursus honorum*, the path of honor. Romans were expected to boast in their accomplishments in order to advance up that path.
- Two examples of this socially acceptable boasting are from Caesar Augustus and Hermogenes. Augustus boasted of his own achievements in military might and triumph. Hermogenes taught students how to praise leaders—this shows what traits leaders were expected to boast in.
- The Weak are reflecting the Roman culture by boasting in their election privilege. Paul responds that Gentiles, through faith, could also gain the Jewish election privilege.
- Gentiles could live out the "Torah of faith" just like the Jews could, and God justifies both the circumcised and the uncircumcised on the basis of faith.
- A question Paul heard over and over from Jews was whether faith overthrows the law. Paul says, no, he upholds the law. However, "The law was never given to justify; the law was given to turn sins into Sin and to reveal Israel's culpability" (129).
- "Turning away from the status and advantage of Torah works and turning toward God in Christ through the Spirit *by faith* and by the faithfulness of Christ both was the ultimate form of observing Torah and led through that same Spirit to living out the Torah" (129).

Chapter 18: The Third Question—Abraham, Faith, and Advantage (4:1-25)

- Paul is asking these questions, but he's putting them in the mouth of the Judge, a representative of the Weak in Rome.
- The Judge thinks the Strong need to convert fully to covenant-keeping, boundary-marker-observing Judaism in order to be faithful to God.
- The third question is a development and restatement of the previous two questions about advantage. This round adds in Abraham. Did

Abraham, their physical ancestor, become righteous by works, specifically circumcision or sacrifice?

- Paul's reason for answering these questions is lived theology—theology for the sake of solving the tension between the Weak and the Strong in the Roman house churches by bringing them into Peace with each other.
- How does Abraham come into this? "Abrahamic faith defines the breadth of the new people of God—*anyone, no matter their status*, who has faith like Abraham, the distinguishing feature of this family, is part of the family" (132).
- Paul looks chronologically at God's work with Abraham. In Genesis 15, God makes a covenant with Abraham by faith, which comes before circumcision in Genesis 17: faith *then* works.
- Paul shows through the Scriptures that it is Abraham's faith that is reckoned to him as righteousness.
- Paul answers the Advantage Question with Two Torahs: of works (4:2, 4) and of faith (3:27).
- The Torah of works is human achievement in which the Weak could boast and because of which they expected God to reward them.
- The reward God promised to Abraham was a child, leading to many descendants in many nations who would be God's people *by faith*.
- Here the words "works" and "wages" are not about individual salvation but are about God's faithfulness—God's plan to start with Abraham and lead to the Messiah, who would bless all the nations (Gentiles). This means that from the beginning, the faith of Abraham was supposed to lead to the inclusion of the Gentiles, which for the Weak means the Strong.
- The Torah of faith is righteousness given by God incongruously to those who believe.
- The Torah of works blesses only the Weak, while the Torah of faith blesses both Strong and Weak.
- Circumcision for Jews was a physical action for male Jews and for male converts to Judaism, an inherent part of covenant faithfulness. For Paul, circumcision of the heart is what's important, and he highlights that Abraham was justified by faith not by circumcision.
- In this justification, Abraham became the ancestor of all the rest who would be justified by faith (both Jew and Gentile). The blessing of righteousness comes through faith in Jesus.

- It is not Torah that creates the heirs of promise—it is grace. God made the promise to Abraham to make him the father of many nations before Abraham was circumcised and before he sacrificed Isaac, so before he did any works.
- In the same way, it is not Torah observance that brings the Strong into the elect people of God—it is grace. Therefore, the Weak must welcome the Strong because they both have faith leading to righteousness.

Ruins in the Roman forum, near the site of Paul's likely imprisonment in Rome.

Group Discussion Questions

Consider the Weak's boasting in election privilege—which of Hermogenes' points is this most similar to? (See pages 127–128)

Ask each student to present a boast for themselves like that of Augustus. What triumphs in their lives would they like to boast in? If your culture today had a *cursus honorum* like in the Roman culture, who in your class would be furthest along the path of public honor? Why? Is what your culture respects today the same as or different from what the Romans respected? What part does Privilege play in students' successes?

Do you think Paul successfully persuaded his audience of his point that Abraham is righteous by faith and not by works? How do you think the conversations around this point went in the Roman house churches?

If the class is comfortable with it, discuss the practice of circumcision. Why is it practiced or not practiced in their culture today? What are their beliefs about the practice? Do they think it is replaced by baptism as the symbol of the new covenant?

Group Learning Activity Suggestions

Read Genesis 15 together and act out the covenant ceremony between God and Abraham. Instructors could bring in props ahead of time or students could use their imaginations to create props out of classroom items. Dramatically perform the covenant scene.

Look at various opinions on the Binding of Isaac in the Resources section. Assign students to represent various views and debate the interpretation of the story. Or let students respond with their own opinions on interpreting the story.

Bring two large rolls of wrapping paper or newsprint and create two Torah scroll props. On one, write "Torah of faith" and on the other write "Torah of works." Ask students to explain the Torah of faith and the Torah of works and write the attributes of each on the prop scrolls.

RESOURCES FOR FURTHER INFORMATION

- Views and opinions on the sacrifice of Isaac
  http://bit.ly/ChabadIsaac
  http://bit.ly/EvansIsaac
  http://bit.ly/JewishLearningIsaac
  http://bit.ly/ReformIsaac
- More information about midrash
  http://bit.ly/JewishLearningMidrash
- For a recent take on midrash by a Hebrew Bible scholar, look up the book *Womanist Midrash* by Wil Gafney or visit her website.
  https://www.wilgafney.com/
- New Testament scholar Craig Keener on Bible context—the last paragraph is about faith and works in Romans
  http://bit.ly/KeenerPostContext
- How circumcision is viewed and practiced today in Reform Judaism
  http://bit.ly/BritMilahToday

FURTHER BIBLE STUDY

☐ Read Philippians 3:5-9, 1 Corinthians 1:31 and 15:31, 2 Corinthians 1:14, 1 Thessalonians 2:19, and Romans 2:17-23. Further insight into Paul's new perspective on boasting.

☐ Read 1 Maccabees 2:52 and James 2:21-24. Consider Abraham's Torah observance and righteousness in these passages.

Personal Study Questions—Lesson Eleven

Chapter 17

What is the Greco-Roman concept of boasting?

How does this differ from how Christians often view boasting today?

Chapter 18

What are the two Torahs?

What reward did God promise Abraham?

What was the point of circumcision in the Hebrew scriptures?

How does Paul say that Abraham was made righteous?

Quiz Questions—Lesson Eleven

1. Which emperor boasted in the *Res Gestae Divi Augusti*?

    A. Augustus

    B. Nero

    C. Claudius

    D. Tiberius

2. Which is NOT one of the areas of boasting in Hermogenes?

    A. Birth

    B. Deeds

    C. Death

    D. Religion

3. Do we then overthrow the law by this faith?

    A. Absolutely yes!

    B. Certainly!

    C. By no means!

    D. Of course!

True or False

4. Works of the Torah have never justified anyone.

5. Abraham was made righteous because he was willing to sacrifice Isaac.

LESSON TWELVE

CHAPTER 19

BEFORE CLASS

❏ Read Romans 5:12-21 and 8:1-8
❏ Read Chapter 19 (16 pages)
❏ Answer the Personal Study Questions

MAIN TAKEAWAY

Romans 5–8 addresses the Strong. Paul uses language toward All, You, We, and I groups to repeat and reinforce his message about two ways of life. The way of Adam involves Sin and leads to Death. The way of Christ involves Grace and leads to Eternal Life. Jesus defeats Sin and Death in his own death and resurrection, giving liberation to both the Strong and the Weak who live by grace.

TERMS AND DEFINITIONS

Cosmology	The study of the universe, the world, the present age, everything that is created.
Anthropology	The study of human beings.
Christology	The study of Jesus Christ, his person and his work.
Universalism	The belief that Jesus will ultimately save all humans.
Emergence theory	Matthew Croasmun wrote the book *The Emergence of Sin: The Cosmic Tyrant in Romans*, which explores sin/Sin in Romans. In his take on "emergence theory," Croasmun argues that something (individual sin) gives rise to something else (systemic/structural sin) that still further gives rise to Something Else (Sin as a disembodied Agent). That first something is necessary for the second and the Third, but the second and Third are increasingly more than the first. Croasmun says that the Third Something is an

emergent reality known as Sin, a person-like Agent that acts through downward causation upon human structures and persons to produce still more sin. Sin is therefore 1. the supervenient foundation of individual human sinful action, 2. the resulting sinful structures/systems/institutions, and 3. the emergent reality of the disembodied personal Agent Sin that exercises downward causation on those same structures/systems and human individuals upon which It is based.

1. Human **individuals** sin . . .
  2. This leads to **systemic/structural** sin . . .
    3. That leads to **Sin** as a disembodied-but-still-personal Agent Who . . .
  2. Works through/above/beyond **systemic/structural** sin to exercise *downward causation* on the
1. Human **individuals** who sin (and around, and around it goes . . .)

Supervenience   This is the foundation (of human individual sins) on which Sin is ultimately based, but it is not the Agent of Sin itself.

Credit to Scot McKnight and Deacon Godsey for the definitions of emergence theory and supervenience.

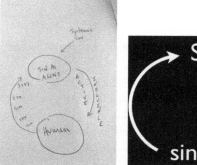 

McKnight's diagrams illustrating Sin in emergence theory (approved by Matthew Croasmun).

Chapter Summaries

Chapter 19: All (5:12-21; 8:1-8)

- "The logic of Romans works like this: Romans 12–16 is the context, 9–11 is a narrative approach to the problem of that context, and Romans 1–4 is Paul's rebuttal of the Weak's claim to priority, elective privilege, and approach to how to live as followers of Jesus in Rome . . . Romans 5–8 *maps Paul's theory of the theological rationale for the lived theology of Romans 12–16*" (142).

- Romans 5–8 seems to have a different audience than 1–4 and the majority of 9–11. This is seen in the lack of Old Testament citations in 5–8, as the sections intended for the Weak were full of quotes from the Hebrew Scriptures.

- Paul wants the lived theology he teaches in Romans to face two directions: toward the public and toward the audience's fellow believers.

- The comprehensive vision for Romans 5–8 tells the entire story of humanity and salvation and transformation into Christoformity.

- Paul traces the line from Adam to Death and the line from Jesus to Life (eternal). Paul attributes advocacy for the Adam-to-Death line to the Judge (Torah Life), while Paul himself advocates for the Jesus-to-Eternal-Life line (Life in the Spirit).

- McKnight pulls out and treats separately four *modes* of Paul's conversation in Romans 5–8: + *Generic / All* (5:12-21; 8:1-8)+ *You* (6:11-23; 8:9-15)+ *We* (5:1-11; 6:1-10; 7:1-6; 8:16-17, 18-39)+ *I* (7:7-25)

- In the All sections, Paul gives a comprehensive cosmic vision about time and creation that is still focused on teaching the Strong and the Weak how to live together in Peace.

- There are Two Ways to live, the Way of Adam / Body of Sin and the Way of Christ / Body of Christ.

- The line of Adam starts with sin, and when Adam sinned, death came in as a consequence and sin spread to all people. Sin was present before Torah, but after Torah sin became Sin (Sin with the uppercase "s" represents a real, acting Self or agent). People who sin end up in the Body of Sin.

- The line of Christ starts with grace, which God spread to all people in the Christ line. People who follow Jesus end up in the Body of Christ.

- There are agents in both Ways, forces that are active and causal.

- In the Adam line, the agents are Sin, Flesh, Torah, and Death, which all come out of human acts of sin. The agents then act on the sinner to cause more sins.
- In the Christ line, the agents are Grace, Torah, Life, and Eternal Life, and they come out of Jesus's acts of obedience. The agents act on the righteous person to cause acts of obedience (righteousness).
- The two different ways create two different cycles: "from sins to Sin and Death, and from Death back to sins, from grace and the obedience of Christ to Life, and from Life back to individual acts of righteousness and justice" (149).
- "Sin . . . is both personal-individual and corporate-systemic, and as such Sin becomes an agent working against the plan of God for humans" (149).
- Each person stands not only alone as an individual but also as a self-in-relation-to-other-selves. Each person is either the Adamic Self or the In-Christ Self.
- Because Sin becomes corporate and systemic, redemption too must be corporate and systemic. This is what McKnight means when he says Paul's theology and anthropology are cosmologies—the studies of God and people encompass the entire universe.
- To bring this discussion back to the Strong and the Weak, the work of Sin and Death in the conflict between them needs to be replaced with the work in Christ of grace and righteousness.
- On original sin, "Paul does not say that all die because all sinned when Adam sinned or in Adam's sin (original guilt)." But rather, "Adam sinned, sin and death entered the world as agents, all die, and all die because all sin/sinned" (150).
- The Weak push the Strong to observe Torah because the Weak believe Torah "was permanent and needed to reveal sin," but Paul shows that sin goes all the way back to Adam, before the Torah. Instead, Paul shows that "Sin as active agent manipulates the Torah into a provocation of sin" (151). The Strong do not have the Torah, but they sin also. Sin and redemption are both for the Weak and the Strong.
- Romans 8:1-8 seems to be directed to the Strong. To them, it is good news to hear that Sin has captured Torah and Flesh has weakened it—this means they don't have to observe Torah to be faithful; rather, they need to live by the Spirit.

- "To deal with Flesh, Christ had to come in the flesh to destroy the Flesh (8:3)" (152). Flesh is a problem for both Jews and Gentiles—all humans.
- In our time, as the present age and the age to come overlap, we live in Christ by the Spirit but sometimes still give in to the Flesh.
- Jesus defeats the enemies (Sin, Flesh, and Death) through offering himself as a sin offering and through his resurrection. Now all humans who are allegiant to Jesus can be transformed by the Spirit, not by Torah observance, into people of righteousness. They move from the Adam way to the Christ way.
- The words in Romans 8 about no condemnation seem to be directed at the Strong, since the Strong are being condemned by the Weak.
- The Generic addresses in Romans 5–8 show that both Strong and Weak should and can follow the Torah of Spirit in Christ and are no longer bound to the Torah captured by Sin and the Flesh. Following the Torah of Spirit leads to Peace for All.

Group Discussion Questions

What are the differences between personal and corporate and systemic sin? How do you see personal sin exhibited around you? How do you see systemic sin acting in your culture?

What does liberation in Christ mean to you?

What do you think about condemnation? How can Paul's words about "no condemnation" work to bring freedom from sin's tyranny into your life?

Group Learning Activity Suggestions

Read the article about original sin and science from BioLogos (in the Resources section). How does science interact with faith? How do theories of human origin intersect with theories of original sin and atonement?

Ask several students to work together to recreate the Two Ways chart from page 145 onto a white board or roll of paper. Then ask other students to explain the content of this lesson by pointing at items on the chart while talking through it. If you have any students in your class who enjoy drawing, ask them to illustrate the Two Ways on the board.

Look through the list of songs based on Romans 5–8 in the Resources section. Choose some that you think your class will know and sing them together.

RESOURCES FOR FURTHER INFORMATION

- BioLogos on original sin and evolution
  http://bit.ly/BioLogosSin
- More about emergence theory and supervenience
  http://bit.ly/StanfordSupervenience
  http://bit.ly/EmergenceSupervenience
- 2 Baruch online
  http://bit.ly/2Baruch
- Extensive overview of John Barclay on "grace" on McKnight's blog
  http://bit.ly/BarclayJesusCreed
- Songs and hymns based on verses in Romans 5–8, arranged
  verse by verse
  http://bit.ly/SongsRomans5-8

FURTHER BIBLE STUDY

❏ Read 2 Baruch 54:19 about Adam. Find a copy of this noncanonical
book online (URL is in the Resources section).

Personal Study Questions—Lesson Twelve

Who is the audience for Romans 5–8?

How does McKnight lay out the logic of Romans in each section? (See page 142.)

Romans 12–16:

Romans 9–11:

Romans 1–4:

Romans 5–8:

What are the two lines/Ways Paul traces?

Which agent appears in both Ways?

What are the four modes of conversation Paul employs in Romans 5–8?

1.
2.
3.
4.

Quiz Questions—Lesson Twelve

1. Which is NOT one of the four modes of conversation Paul uses?

    A. All
    B. We
    C. Y'all
    D. You

2. Which is a placard on the Adam Way?

    A. Grace
    B. Righteousness
    C. Death
    D. Eternal Life

3. What turns sin into Sin?

    A. Death
    B. Flesh
    C. Torah
    D. Evil

True or False

4. Torah is in both the Way of Adam and the Way of Christ.

5. Everyone in the Way of Christ becomes siblings.

LESSON THIRTEEN

CHAPTER 20

BEFORE CLASS

❏ Read Romans 5:1-11, 6:1-23, 7:1-6, and 8:9-39
❏ Read Chapter 20 (9 pages)
❏ Answer the Personal Study Questions

MAIN TAKEAWAY

When Paul speaks to "You," he means the Weak who are under the law themselves and want to bring the Strong under the law. When he speaks to the "We" people, he means the Strong, and he often counts himself among them. There is a Personal Way added to the Way of Adam and the Way of Christ. This is the way of salvation for each person, both Strong and Weak, that leads them through baptism and transformation into Christoformity. This is the theology that supports the lived theology Paul gives them in Romans 14–15.

TERMS AND DEFINITIONS

Ordo salutis   This phrase comes from the Latin for "order of salvation." Lutheranism first used this idea in the 1700s. It refers to a sequential order of steps of human salvation, though the exact steps and order are different in various systems.

CHAPTER SUMMARIES

Chapter 20: You and We (6:11-23; 8:9-15; 5:1-11; 6:1-10; 7:1-6; 8:16-17, 18-39)

- The You passages are in 6:11-23 and 8:9-15. They follow the same general ideas looked at previously but with more direct language: "you" and "yourselves."

- These statements speak more specifically about sin—don't be slaves to sin but be subject to God, which might have connected with the slaves and former slaves in the churches (again, knowing the context of the house churches and who attended them helps move the rhetoric of Romans from the abstract to the concrete).
- People (You) are transformed into righteousness by the Holy Spirit.
- Who are the You people? McKnight concludes they, those "under the law," are the Weak who are trying to get the Strong to observe Torah.
- The We passages are in 5:1-11; 6:1-10; 7:1-6; 8:16-17, 18-39. These sections build a Personal Way in addition to the Adam Way and the Christ Way.
- Romans has repetitive ideas in various sections.
- The Weak push More Torah and the Strong push No Torah, but Paul pushes More Spirit.
- Who are the We people? McKnight concludes it's the Strong, and Paul frequently identifies himself among them.
- There are six rip-roaring themes in these sections that must be untangled and addressed separately while examining the Personal Way.

  1. The former condition of all humans: before Jesus came, each human and all of creation was captive to Sin and Evil, and Jesus redeems everything through grace.
  2. The revelation of God in Christ to rescue humans from sins, Sin, Flesh, and Death: God's love leads to God's gift of grace. Jesus's death and resurrection broke the enemy power and provided the way for humans to move from Adam's line to Christ's line. Jesus now intercedes for us after the ascension. The gift redeems people in the direction of Christoformity, so they can live out love of God and others.
  3. The gift and its benefits that come to humans in Christ: God's gift offers many benefits and is given regardless of Privilege (social privilege of Strong and election privilege of Weak). God's redemption is *"cosmic, personal liberation unto Christoformity"* (163).
  4. The new condition of life with the gift: Baptism brings people into the new Life after they die with Christ. The Jewish believers died to the law and became alive in the Spirit, which obeys even more than the Torah. The Strong die to the desire to go on sinning, highlighting grace.
  5. The human participation in the gift: Both Strong and Weak join in the redemption, transformation, and liberation by faith, hope, love, and baptism. Christoformity shows in the suffering both

endure—the Weak in paying taxes and the Strong in giving up their social status. "Participation . . . is a full participation from the moment of faith/baptism to the end of life. The obsession at times in Christianity with the moment of decision runs against the grain of how Paul understands participation in Christ" (168).

6. The future in Christ: In the age to come, all the believers will experience glorification and full Christoformity. In eternity, all will be full of love for God and each other.

- In this section, "we find the theological roots for what he must tell the Strong in Romans 14–15 about how to live" (169).
- "To love God is to be ruggedly, affectively committed to God, to be present to God, to be an advocate for God, and to be transformed by God's presence into Christoformity" (167–8).
- Righteousness is a gift of God as an extension of God's character that transforms humans into a life of righteous actions, reciprocated back to God as a gift.

Group Discussion Questions

For those in your class who have been baptized and would like to share, invite them to tell the stories of their baptisms. Where and when were they baptized? What did the experience mean to them?

Why do you think those who have chosen the Way of Christ still sin sometimes?

Group Learning Activity Suggestions

McKnight defines what it means to love God in a biblical way on pages 167–8. This is an outgrowth of his work over the past few years on biblical love—the way God loves us and the way we should love each other. View some earlier iterations of this work and compare them to this (URLs to a video and blog post in the Resources section).

Using the framework of faith, hope, and love, create a chart of how humans participate in God's gifts. See page 167 for Bible references. Look them up and read them together.

Look up the song "No Longer Slaves" from Bethel Music, the lyrics or the music video or a live performance video. Listen together then discuss how the song lyrics relate to the themes of this lesson (slavery, liberation, becoming part of God's family).

RESOURCES FOR FURTHER INFORMATION

- Three different maps for *ordo salutis*
  http://bit.ly/CARMOrdo
- Various views on baptism in different Christian traditions
  http://bit.ly/baptismtheology
- McKnight on biblical love (earlier work)
  http://bit.ly/McKnightLoveSeedbed (video)
  http://bit.ly/JesusCreedLove (blog post)

FURTHER BIBLE STUDY

❑ Read Acts 2:38, 8:16, and 22:16; Galatian 3:27; 1 Corinthians 12:13; Titus 3:5; Hebrews 10:22; and 1 Peter 3:21. Look at what these verses say about baptism.

PERSONAL STUDY QUESTIONS—LESSON THIRTEEN

What does it mean to be glorified?

List the gifts from God on page 163.

Which one most stands out to you, and why?

Explain "righteousness" based on page 164.

How does McKnight explain what it means to love God on pages 167–8?

Quiz Questions—Lesson Thirteen

1. The idea of offering themselves to God in Romans 6:13 is repeated in which later chapter?

    A.   12

    B.   13

    C.   14

    D.   15

2. Paul calls for:

    A.   More Torah

    B.   More Sacrifice

    C.   More Faith

    D.   More Spirit

3. Which is NOT one of the gifts of God listed on page 163?

    A.   Christ's intercession

    B.   Power

    C.   Glory

    D.   Redemption

True or False

4. Justification comes through works of the Torah.

5. Righteousness and justification come from the same root word in Greek.

LESSON FOURTEEN

CHAPTER 21, CONCLUSION

BEFORE CLASS

❑ Read Chapter 21 (7 pages)
❑ Read the Conclusion (3 pages)
❑ Answer the Personal Study Questions

MAIN TAKEAWAY

The "I" in Romans 7 is the personification of someone who tries to keep Torah but can't. That's because Torah was never intended to cause transformation into righteousness but rather to show God's will and Israel's sin. It is Christ through the Spirit who liberates people from all forces of evil so they can live by the Spirit, which surpasses living by the Torah. Spirit life leads to Peace in the empire.

TERMS AND DEFINITIONS

Prosopopoeia   This is a literary or rhetorical device that gives a writer or speaker the opportunity to assign thoughts to a made-up character, often a stereotype. The character can say things differently from the content creator, allowing them to dialogue or argue with each other. Here, the character is the Judge.

CHAPTER SUMMARIES

Chapter 21: I

- Who is the I person? "The 'I' of Romans 7 is someone exploring transformation through the Torah but fails miserably at observing the Torah" (172). McKnight refers back to Romans 2 and calls this character in Romans 7 "the Judge."

101

- Paul perhaps delivered this same message in all his churches because he often saw Jewish believers trying to get Gentile converts to observe Torah as part of their conversion. This passage in Romans 7 could be Paul's standard argument about why Gentiles don't need to follow Torah.
- Paul says Torah was temporary and its goal was to show that sin is transgression, to make sin into Sin. Torah was not about making people Christoform.
- The Judge says Torah reveals sin, Torah plus Sin brings Death, and Torah makes sin become Sin. Still, the Torah is good and spiritual. "Torah only becomes an instrument of Death because of Sin and Flesh" (176). Sin dwells in the Judge and is a tyrant over the Judge.
- Torah was never intended to cause transformation into righteousness but rather to show God's will and Israel's sin.
- Christ through the Spirit liberates people from all forces of evil so they can live by the Spirit—there is no condemnation for them because they are free from the law of sin and are now under the law of the Spirit of life. The lived theology result is that they can live out Peace with each other.

Conclusion: Reading Romans Forwards, in Brief

- "The intent of Romans is Christoformity in both Jewish and Gentile believers, roughly, then, the Weak and the Strong" (179).
- By starting with the context in Romans 14–15 and seeing the conflict over table fellowship and kosher food between the Strong (Roman) and Weak (Jewish) believers, readers can understand Romans in new ways.
- Romans 1–4 becomes about Jewish believers judging Gentile believers over Torah observance, not about all individuals sinning and needing to be saved.
- Romans 5–8 is the theological basis for solution to the conflict Paul gives in 14–15. "The relationship of Romans 5–8 to Romans 12–16 is not theology and practice but lived theology and theology for that lived theology" (180).
- Romans 12–16 can be summed up with "Christoformity." Both sides of the conflict need to give up their Privilege and Power to live in Peace as they welcome each other.

In the Basilica of Saint Paul Outside the Walls, outside Rome, is a case that holds what are purported to be Paul's chains from his Roman imprisonment.

The Abbey of the Three Fountains, outside the walls of Rome, is traditionally held to be the site of Paul's execution. The path he walked and the column where he was beheaded are protected there.

GROUP DISCUSSION QUESTIONS

How has your understanding of Romans changed over the course of this study?

How has your spiritual life changed during this class?

What do you plan to do differently in your church life as a result of studying Romans backwards?

GROUP LEARNING ACTIVITY SUGGESTIONS

McKnight imagines that Paul had to answer the same questions from Jewish believers everywhere he went. Expand on this idea as a class and make a cheat sheet for Paul to carry to meetings with Jewish believers as he continues on his missionary journeys.

Watch the two Bible Project videos on Romans together then discuss. How does their presentation differ from McKnight's? How is it similar? How do you find yourself tracking with the videos differently from how you might have before you took this class? Do the videos introduce you to any ideas you hadn't considered in your Romans study so far?

The conclusion offers a challenge to the American church, the context in which and to which McKnight is writing. "The message of Romans is that the Weak and the Strong of our day—and I say now what I have not said, that everyone thinks that they are the Strong and that the other is the Weak—must surrender their claims to privilege and hand them over to Christoformity" (180–1). Give the two articles by women of color in the Resources section to your students to examine how Privilege and Power play out in the American church today. Discuss how you can each work to become Christoform in order to live into Peace.

Prepare the students for your closing activity next week. You will be reading Romans together—forward, this time! Assign a large section of Romans to each student. They will be responsible to study that section and prepare to perform it for the class in a dramatic reading such as Phoebe might have done. Ask them to read the post about letter performance listed in the Resources section. Recall the ideas throughout the book about whom Phoebe might have been looking at—pointedly—in each section. Encourage the class to prepare to respond to each reader as well. You could pre-divide the room into the Strong and Weak sections for the audience.

FOR THE INSTRUCTORS

If you will be giving a final exam, use the quiz questions to create a test or write your own. Give the students an idea of what the exam will focus on so they can study. For quiz answers, see Appendix B.

For sample essay topics you could use for an essay test or for a paper due at the end of the class term, see Appendix C.

RESOURCES FOR FURTHER INFORMATION

- Bible Project video on Romans—two parts
  https://thebibleproject.com/explore/romans/
- Blog post by McKnight summarizing the work of William Shiell on New Testament letter performance
  http://bit.ly/PerformingPaul
- Christena Cleveland on Privilege
  http://bit.ly/ClevelandPrivilege
- Kaitlin Curtice on Power, specifically using the Bible to oppress people
  http://bit.ly/CurticePower

FURTHER BIBLE STUDY

❑ Read your assigned section of Romans multiple times to prepare for your performance. Consider listening to several different audio Bibles of your section as well. Try to get familiar enough with it that you will be able to look up from your Bible to make eye contact. How will you stand? What gestures will you use? Where in the audience will you look?

PERSONAL STUDY QUESTIONS—LESSON FOURTEEN

Chapter 21

Why is there no condemnation for those in Christ?

What is the purpose of the Torah?

What is Paul's reason for using the speech-in-character device?

Conclusion

McKnight says on page 181, "The message shouts to the American church that its classism, its racism, its sexism, and its materialism are like the Strong's social-status claims and the Weak's boundaried behaviors." Where do social-status claims and or boundaried behaviors show up in your life?

How will you address them and change in order to welcome your siblings better?

Study the chapter summaries, main points, and previous quiz questions to prepare for the exam as well as any study guides your teacher hands out.

LESSON FIFTEEN

EXAM AND ROMANS PERFORMANCE .

BEFORE CLASS

❑ Study for the exam
❑ Prepare to perform your assigned chapter of Romans

EXAM

Administer the exam at the beginning of the class period.

ROMANS PERFORMANCE

Enjoy learning together as you hear all of Romans at one time, just as the Roman house churches may have heard it. Consider using costumes and a prop parchment for the letter from Paul. May Romans challenge you, encourage you, and bring you into a life of Christoform Peace together with your siblings around the table.

Rita Bakunda portrays Deacon Phoebe in a performance of Romans 9 at Damascus Road International Church in Maastricht, Netherlands.

ACKNOWLEDGMENTS

Thank you to all my siblings who breathed Peace into my life while I worked on this study guide:

+ My husband, Matthew Miller, for holding up my arms and sacrificing his work for the sake of mine
+ My children, Katherine, Joshua, Estel, Providence, and Iunia, for being patient with me
+ Laura Pintus, Rosie Roys, Judith Dik, Christine Lunders, Jessica Markink, Mariam Shokralla, and Victoria Henshaw for helping care for my children
+ Matthew Lunders and Jessica Markink for the cookies, conversations, care, and concern, and together with Renske Letema, Lucile Lesueur, Praveen Sam, Rosie Roys, Simona Dumitrescu, Josh Campbell, Augusta Alele, and Rita Bakunda in our DRx class for letting me practice teaching biblical interpretation for the church with you
+ Karen Burk and Abbie Daley for saving my bacon
+ My MANT '16 cohort at Northern Seminary for welcoming me to the table as we've learned Romans backwards together—I'm going to miss having the greatest Monday nights of our lives with you after we graduate
+ My classmates and our new friends on the Footsteps of Paul trip for the lifelong memories
+ Deacon Godsey and Tommy Phillips for reviewing some of these lessons and improving them
+ The great team at Baylor University Press for making this study guide a reality
+ Scot McKnight and Cherith Fee Nordling for giving love through their generous advocacy for me

APPENDIX A:
PLAN FOR 8 WEEKS OF CLASSES

LESSON ONE: CONTEXT—THE RECIPIENTS OF THE LETTER
    Read Preface, Introduction, Chapter 1, Chapter 2, Chapter 3, Chapter 4
    (28 pages of reading)

LESSON TWO: LIVED THEOLOGY IS CHRISTOFORMITY
    Read Chapter 5, Chapter 6, Chapter 7, Chapter 8, Chapter 9 (25 pages
    of reading)
    Read Romans 12–16

LESSON THREE: WEAK AND STRONG
    Read Chapter 10, Chapter 11, Chapter 12 (31 pages of reading)
    Read Romans 9–11.

LESSON FOUR: THE BEGINNING OF THE LETTER
    Read Chapter 13, Chapter 14, Chapter 15 (22 pages of reading)

LESSON FIVE: THE THREE QUESTIONS
    Read Chapter 16, Chapter 17, Chapter 18 (22 pages of reading)
    Read Romans 1–4

LESSON SIX: US
    Read Chapter 19, Chapter 20 (30 pages of reading)

LESSON SEVEN: CONCLUSION
    Chapter 21, Conclusion (10 pages of reading)
    Read Romans 5–8
    Test prep and review

LESSON EIGHT
    Exam and Romans performance

APPENDIX B: QUIZ ANSWERS

1. Which is NOT a major theme in *Reading Romans Backwards*?
C. Prosperity
2. Who carried Paul's letter to the Roman house churches?
B. Phoebe
3. Claudius was the emperor of Rome when Paul wrote his letter. **F**
4. Paul uses the language of siblings to talk about relationships in the church. **T**
5. Romans is a theological treatise about individual salvation. **F**

LESSON TWO

1. Where in Rome did the Christians likely live?
B. Trastevere, Via Appia, Aventine, Via Lata/Flaminia
2. Who was NOT a prominent Christian woman greeted in Romans 16?
D. Susanna
3. In what year did Claudius expel the Jewish believers from Rome? **A. 49**
4. The Jesus-followers in Rome at the time Paul wrote his letter were mostly Gentile. **T**
5. The number of Christians in Rome in the first century was likely over 200. **F**

LESSON THREE

1. The arguments between the Strong and the Weak in Romans 14–15 have to do with: **A. Food laws, holy days, circumcision**
2. Which of these is NOT a trait of the Weak? **C. Do not keep the Torah**
3. Which of these is a trait of the Strong?
D. Have social status in Rome
4. Paul's mission was to plant churches made of Jewish believers in Jesus. **F**
5. Paul was a Pharisee and a Zealot. **T**

Lesson Four

1. Two aspects of embodied God orientation are:

A. Sacrifice and prayer

2. Which of these was NOT one of the six points about embodied sacrifice?

B. Sacrifice is seen best in generous financial giving

3. Which of these was NOT one of the six points about prayer?

D. Paul prays to the Holy Spirit

4. Paul tells the Weak and Strong to keep thinking highly of themselves. **F**

5. Paul says the spiritual gifts are for the benefit of the ones who possess them. **F**

Lesson Five

1. Which of these is NOT a theme of body-of-Christ orientation?

C. Civil obedience

2. What was the first priority when looking at public orientation?

A. Love

3. Which of these was a strategy for loving neighbors outside the church?

D. Empathizing

4. God's covenant is made first with Israel and then, through them, also with the Gentiles. **T**

5. A public orientation would probably have been harder for the Strong than for the Weak. **F**

Lesson Six

1. How many questions does Paul batter the Weak with? **D. 21**

2. What five topics does this lesson look at in Romans 9–11?

B. Persons, narrative comparisons, events, texts, questions

3. Romans 9–11 answers this question:

A. Who are the gospel agents in God's redemptive plan?

4. The question of the Weak is: "Is not Israel the elect people of God?" **T**

5. The question of the Strong is: "Is it not the case that God has moved from Israel to the Gentiles in salvation through the cosmic Lord Jesus?" **T**

Lesson Seven

1. Which one is NOT one of the three characters in Matthew Bates's perspective on 10:5–13? **D. The Judge**

2. What do "works of the law" mean in Romans 9–11?

A. Observing food laws, keeping Sabbath, practicing circumcision

3. Which is NOT one of the three key terms in this lesson?

C. Welcome

4. The three-in-one problem is (1) Israel, works, Torah as boundary markers; (2) faith and Messiah; and (3) election privilege. **F**

5. The Messiah is the stumbling stone. **T**

LESSON EIGHT

1. Which of these is NOT one of the five themes in this lesson?

D. Circumcision

2. Which object is part of an analogy Paul makes about the correlation of the Strong?

C. Dough

3. God is jealous when the people are:

D. All of the above

4. The Strong could lose their place on the rootstock by their disobedience. **T**

5. All Israel will be saved. **T**

LESSON NINE

1. Which one is NOT one of the four gospel themes in this lesson?

C. The gospel saves first Gentiles and second Jews

2. The prophet Paul quotes who contrasts the proud with the righteous who live by faith is:

A. Habakkuk

3. Paul is not ashamed of: **C. The gospel**

4. The term "Messiah" could appeal to the Strong and "Lord" to the Weak. **F**

5. The phrase "Through faith for faith" is clear and has been consistently interpreted. **F**

LESSON TEN

1. Which is NOT a descriptor of the Judge?

C. Does not know the Torah

2. Which IS one of the three rhetorical turnabouts?

A. The Judge is a hypocrite

3. The second of the three principal question is about: **C. Boasting**

4. The limited statements about the Weak/the Judge have been taken to be universal statements about all Jews. **T**

5. We are saved by faith and judged by works. **T**

Lesson Eleven

1. Which emperor boasted in the *Res Gestae Divi Augusti*?
A. Augustus
2. Which is NOT one of the areas of boasting in Hermogenes?
D. Religion
3. Do we then overthrow the law by this faith?
C. By no means!
4. Works of the Torah have never justified anyone. **T**
5. Abraham was made righteous because he was willing to sacrifice Isaac. **F**

Lesson Twelve

1. Which is NOT one of the four modes of conversation Paul uses?
C. Y'all
2. Which is a placard on the Adam Way?
C. Death
3. What turns sin into Sin?
C. Torah
4. Torah is in both the Way of Adam and the Way of Christ. **T**
5. Everyone in the Way of Christ becomes siblings. **T**

Lesson Thirteen

1. The idea of offering themselves to God in Romans 6:13 is repeated in which later chapter?
A. 12
2. Paul calls for:
D. More Spirit
3. Which is NOT one of the gifts of God listed on page 163?
B. Power
4. Justification comes through works of the Torah. **F**
5. Righteousness and justification come from the same root word in Greek. **T**

APPENDIX C: ESSAY TOPICS

- Describe the context of the book of Romans. To whom was written? When? For what purpose?
- Who were the Strong and the Weak in Romans, and what was the main conflict between them?
- What did Paul mean when he told the Roman Christians to be subject to governing authorities?
- How do spiritual gifts lead to unity in the church?
- Who were the "elect"? What does election mean?
- How and why does Paul reimagine the story of Israel?
- What is the purpose of Paul's rhetorical strategy of questioning?
- How is it possible for there to be no condemnation for those who are in Christ?
- What is the purpose of the Torah?
- Should Gentile converts to Christianity observe the Torah?
- Who are the sinners in Romans 1?
- Is Romans about individual salvation? Why or why not?

To encourage imagination in your students, consider asking them to write a story in addition to essays and papers. Here are some possible story ideas:

- Write a biography about one of the recipients greeted in Romans 16. Include a description of her or his response to Paul's letter.
- Write a letter back to Paul from either a member of the Strong or the Weak.
- Write a narrative about one of the Old Testament characters in Romans 9. How did they see their place in salvation history?

APPENDIX D: FURTHER READING

This bibliography is focused primarily on readable and inexpensive books on Romans, including some McKnight has used in his Romans courses at Northern Seminary. These would be good books for an undergraduate course, a Sunday school class, a small group, or personal study. There is a longer and more thorough bibliography with a more academic focus in *Reading Romans Backwards*.

Further Reading on Romans

Blount, Brian K., Cain Hope Felder, Clarice J. Martin, and Emerson B. Powery, eds. *True to Our Native Land: An African American New Testament Commentary*. Minneapolis, Minnesota: Fortress Press, 2007.

Finger, Reta Halteman. *Roman House Churches for Today: A Practical Guide for Small Groups*. Grand Rapids, Michigan: Eerdmans, 2007.

Gaventa, Beverly Roberts. *When in Romans: An Invitation to Linger with the Gospel According to Paul*. Grand Rapids, Michigan: Baker Academic, 2016.

Gooder, Paula. *Phoebe: A Story*. Downers Grove, Illinois: IVP Academic, 2018.

Lancaster, Sarah Heaner. *Romans*. Belief: A Theological Commentary on the Bible. Louisville, Kentucky: Westminster John Knox Press, 2015.

Oakes, Peter. *Reading Romans in Pompeii: Paul's Letter at Ground Level*. Minneapolis, Minnesota: Fortress Press, 2013.

Sermons on Romans

McKnight, Scot, and Joseph B. Modica, eds. *Preaching Romans: Four Perspectives*. Grand Rapids, Michigan: Eerdmans, 2019.

Rutledge, Fleming. *Not Ashamed of the Gospel: Sermons from Paul's Letter to the Romans*. Grand Rapids, Michigan: Eerdmans, 2007.

ADDITIONAL COMMENTARIES ON ROMANS

Note: these are more academic than the previous books.

Bird, Michael F. *Romans*. The Story of God Bible Commentary. Grand Rapids, Michigan: Zondervan, 2016.

Fitzmyer, Joseph A. *Romans: A New Translation with Introduction and Commentary*. Anchor Yale Bible 33. New Haven, Connecticut: Yale University Press, 1993.

Jewett, Robert. *Romans: A Short Commentary*. Minneapolis, Minnesota: Fortress Press, 2013.

Keck, Leander E. *Romans*. Abingdon New Testament Commentaries. Nashville, Tennessee: Abingdon Press, 2005.

GENERAL READING ON PAUL

Dunn, James D. G. *The Theology of Paul the Apostle*. Grand Rapids, Michigan: Eerdmans, 1997.

Gorman, Michael J. *Becoming the Gospel: Paul, Participation, and Mission*. Grand Rapids, Michigan: Eerdmans, 2015.

Sanders, E. P. *Paul: The Apostle's Life, Letters, and Thought*. Minneapolis, Minnesota: Fortress Press, 2015.

Wright, N. T. *Paul: A Biography*. San Francisco, California: HarperOne, 2018.

APPENDIX E: "OUR SISTER PHOEBE"

AN ORIGINAL SHORT STORY BY BECKY CASTLE MILLER

Paul drove me crazy. And he made me laugh. Some days, he did both.

I winced when he tossed papyrus on the floor, and I hoped the dust wouldn't stick to the ink. Tertius picked it up and blew on it without ceremony. He was used to this.

"You copied from the wrong draft, Tertius!" Paul stopped pacing and rubbed his bald head with both hands until it shone in the lamplight. "I said, 'bear with the failings of the weak,' not 'be patient with the weaknesses of those who don't have power.'"

I jumped in and argued, "But we agreed on the other version yesterday! 'Those without power.' The power differential matters!"

"Of course it does, Phoebe!" Paul said. "That's what I mean by 'Strong' and 'Weak'!"

He was so particular about each word. I'd stopped counting how many iterations of this section of the letter we had gone through. "That's not clear enough!" I heard my own voice sounding tight with intensity. I suggested a tamer version of my preference: "What if you say, 'those lacking influence'?"

Timothy spoke up from the table in the corner. "How about 'the minority'? Just be explicit: the Jewish minority needs the Gentile majority to support them in their convictions instead of pressuring them into doing things the Gentile way."

Tertius looked from the papyrus in his hands to Timothy to me to Paul. He knew I held the strings of the purse that paid him. But Timothy was currently his roommate. But Paul was in charge—we all knew that. Tertius opened his mouth and closed it again. He was always methodical with his phrasing, whether writing or speaking. "Mister Paul ... even though you're a Jew, you're in the position of the Strong. You have freedom of conscience, and you have the powerful position of a man with apostolic authority." He paused and bit his lower lip. "Maybe you should listen to those who are female and those who are young on this—they know better what it means to be powerless."

Timothy and I both turned our heads to Paul.

One corner of his mouth twitched. "Well said, Tertius. I stand corrected. Let's go with 'those who don't have power.'" Paul could debate a position with ferocity, but he was quick to change his mind when convinced by an opponent.

My shoulders relaxed.

Paul laughed. "Tertius, you are not only an excellent scribe and editor, you are also a wise mediator. I have half a mind to send you to the Roman situation instead of Phoebe. She might incite riot with her fiery opinions." He caught my eyes, and his crinkled at the corners. I knew he liked my zeal, even when he gave me grief for it.

Tertius started collecting the papyri from Timothy's spot at the table. "I'll finish writing this part soon, Mister Paul. I just need to mix more ink. Would you like to read it after the assembly?"

"Tomorrow morning is soon enough. We still have a week before Phoebe leaves."

The main door flew open, and Gaius squeezed through into my front room. "Greetings, brothers and sister! How goes the work?"

Paul started speaking a greeting, but the last half was muffled into Gaius's hearty embrace. I shook my head. It was as if they hadn't seen each other in months. Really it had only been a few days, since Paul had moved from Gaius's large home in Corinth over to mine in Cenchreae. I had come home to finish preparations for my journey, and Paul, Timothy, and Tertius had followed me because the letter still wasn't done.

Gaius eyed Paul's many bags spilling out onto the floor, right where we needed to fit the twenty people who would show up for the assembly at any moment. "Phoebe, how do you put up with him? What's that you all were writing about *welcoming strangers* into your home the other day?"

Paul grinned. "I believe I said, 'bless those who persecute you . . . bless and don't curse them.'"

Timothy stood up and came over to repack Paul's belongings. "And don't pay back anyone for their evil actions with evil actions . . . to the best of your ability, live at peace with everyone." Riffing on the contents of the letter had become a standard part of our collective humor that had helped keep us sane all winter as the letter slowly took shape.

I knelt to help Timothy. Paul couldn't bend down very easily; it pulled the scar tissue on his back.

Paul kicked a cloak toward the pile. "And if your enemy is hungry . . . feed him?"

I stood, pursing my lips to hold back a chuckle. No matter how tense the serious debates became, Paul could always amuse me with a repurposed or out-of-context quote. "If that means it's time for dinner, I agree. I'll call the slaves to lay the food. Everyone will be here soon."

After the fellowship meal, I lifted the bread, a large, circular loaf, decorated with patterns cut into the dough. Though I had asked Paul to honor us by leading the remembrance, he had deferred to me as the assembly's deacon. I recited what Paul had taught me, copying his inflection: "On the night he was betrayed, the Lord Jesus took bread. After giving thanks, he broke it, saying, 'This is my body which is for you. Do this in remembrance of me.'" I tore the loaf in half, then ripped off a small piece as I had watched him do. I had developed my own addition to the practice of passing the bread. I walked to each person in the room, handing out the pieces. One for the craftworker in the adjoining shop. "Albus, the body of the Christ, broken for you."

One for his tenant who lived upstairs. "Florus, the body of the Christ, broken for you."

One for our homeless friend who took turns sleeping in our main rooms. "Quartus, the body of the Christ, broken for you."

One for the city treasurer. "Erastus, the body of the Christ, broken for you."

One for the kitchen slave who had baked the bread herself. "Anthusa, the body of the Christ, broken for you."

One for me. I held the bright flesh of the bread in my dark fingers and examined it. Broken for each of us, pieces from the same loaf. Members of the same body.

The work continued. And continued. Tertius's patience was lasting longer than mine. "My ship sails in three days, Paul." I gritted my teeth. "Have you finished the conclusion?"

Timothy laughed. "Which one? So far he's written four different benedictions, and he wants to include all of them."

Paul smiled and redirected the conversation. "Do you want to hear what I said about you, Phoebe?"

I rubbed the back of my neck. "Only if it's nice things."

"Very nice things. Tertius?"

Tertius found the line and read: "I'm introducing our sister Phoebe to you, who is a deacon of the church in Cenchreae. Welcome her in the Lord in a way that is worthy of God's people, and give her whatever she needs from you, because she herself has been a sponsor of many people, including many of you."

"Thank you, brother Paul," I said. "That's kind of you. Don't you think it's a little heavy handed, though? I know our friends are grateful for the ways I've been able to help them in the past. We don't need to rub it in their faces."

"That's a fair point," Paul said. "How about 'a sponsor of many people, *myself* included'?"

"I like that. And it was gladly done."

Paul called Timothy over to help him review the list of greetings to make sure they hadn't left anyone out. They stood together by the window, examining the papyrus. "Hermas, Philologus, Julia, Nereus, and . . . what is the name of his sister?"

Timothy pulled on his ear and tried to remember.

I left them to it and went back to my packing. In addition to Paul's letter, I had documents of my own to carry for my business interests in Rome, not to mention the clothes I would need. Meeting other merchants of high status would require all the right outfits. I hoped none of my belongings would get lost in transit.

I'd never seen a countenance like hers. Junia's face glowed with an inextinguishable light, an eternal flame of confident hope. I'd asked a simple question: "What was he like?" And she had launched into a two-hour tornado of adulation for the risen Jesus. She had seen him in his resurrected body with her own eyes, heard his commission to his students with her own ears, and she had been running after that mission every day for the two decades since his ascension. She and her husband, Andronicus, had planted churches from Jerusalem all the way to Rome, even spending time in prison like Paul, and now they were leading a tiny assembly here. In the capital city of the empire, where apartment buildings and villas overflowed with a million inhabitants, they were two of only thirty thousand Jews, two of only a hundred Christians.

"He's the Good Shepherd, Phoebe. He set the example for how we should lead. As you teach your church, remember to serve." She reached out and clasped my hands as she wound down her spiel. Her fingers were strong though the skin was tough and mottled. "Use these hands to wash their feet. Set aside your status to lift up those without status."

I heard the kinship resemblance with Paul and knew she would be a happy recipient of his letter. She shared the same pastoral concern for the people who met in her home as Paul did. The conflict between the Jewish and Gentile believers was hindering the spreading of the message about Jesus. It was her invitation that brought me to her house today to meet with the various assembly leaders so that we could strategize before I visited their gatherings throughout the week to come. I would be presenting the letter at each of the five assemblies, and the hosts wanted to know what was in it so they could help me anticipate and prepare for the responses I was likely to get. A few other leaders I didn't recognize—people with several different skin colors and clothes that showed their varying social levels—had trickled into the room as Junia had been testifying about Jesus. They were all listening to her with interest and respect.

Andronicus laid a hand on his wife's shoulder to pause her speaking before she ramped up again. "Priscilla and Aquila are at the door, beloved."

I squeezed Junia's warm hands then jumped up to greet my friends. It was so good to see them again, and I looked forward to learning from them, as always. Priscilla had such a gift for clarity, and I had questions saved up for her about teaching in my church. I embraced the couple with kisses—"One from me," I told them, "and one from brother Paul."

Priscilla drew me to sit between her and Aquila. "Tell us, how is he?" Her carefully shaped eyebrows drew together.

"He is as brilliant and annoying as ever." I laughed, and so did they.

"Will he visit us himself?" Aquila asked.

"Yes, he hopes to," I said. "On his way to Spain."

"Spain?" they exclaimed together.

I shrugged. "He has decided that's the direction to go to reach places where they haven't heard of Jesus yet. Now that he has traveled all the way from Jerusalem around to Illyricum, he feels like there isn't any place for him to work in those regions anymore."

"When will he arrive?" Andronicus asked.

"I don't know. First he's going back to Jerusalem to deliver the Gentile offering to the poor there."

Junia chewed on the inside of her cheek. "Does he think they'll welcome him in Jerusalem?"

"Honestly . . . I think he's worried that they won't."

"We will pray for this," she said.

I was about to thank her, assuming she meant she would pray later, when she stood and lifted her hands right then. Andronicus and several others did the same. Junia prayed, "Our Father, we thank you that you have brought Phoebe here safely. We thank you for the good news from Paul. Lead him by the wisdom and power of your Spirit to all the good works you have planned for him. May your people in Jerusalem accept his service and the gift from the Gentiles. Your kingdom come."

Again I heard echoes of Paul in her words and in her enthusiasm.

She clapped and called for her daughter. "Mary! Bring the food, please. Let's eat before we get down to business."

I was curious to see what they would serve. The way the leaders handled their meals together might give me some clues about what to emphasize with the church members.

Mary brought out a pot of lentils then a tray of vegetables—cabbage and lettuce, mostly. Finally a plate of whole smoked fish. I portioned it out with my eyes and realized there wouldn't be enough food to go around. They indicated that I should serve myself first, so I took a small serving of everything, just enough to avoid offending my hostess, but leaving as much as possible for others. Priscilla and Aquila took generous helpings, then Andronicus, Junia, and Mary finished it off. I looked at the other three, who sat without food, and raised an eyebrow. This was the most unusual hospitality practice I had ever witnessed.

The one woman must have noticed my confusion, because she spoke. "We . . . we ate earlier. Um. Hello. I'm Tryphaena."

One of the men added, "We're not particularly hungry. But thank you, Andronicus, for inviting us to meet Phoebe."

"Of course, Asyncritus, you're very welcome," Andronicus said. His previously soft voice now sounded strained. "We thank God for this food." He took a bite, and the other Jews followed his lead.

There was silence while they chewed. I weighed letting it go versus asking the rude question. I decided I had to know what I was in for tomorrow, so I asked. "Do you . . . did you eat before you came . . . on purpose?" No one answered me, so I tried again. "Do you not eat meals together?"

Junia replied first. "We value unity and peace. Our different dietary preferences can make meals challenging. We have found that eating separately is better for our fellowship."

"But . . ." I hated to contradict an apostle, but I had the backing of another apostle in this. "But without a fellowship meal, do you really have fellowship at all?"

"We didn't want to keep arguing about it," the other man said. "The Jews wouldn't give up their superstitions about food, so we agreed to disagree."

Priscilla gripped her cup. "They're not superstitions, Philologus!"

I crunched a celery stalk, and the snapping between my teeth was loud in my ears. If it was like this among the leaders, addressing the assemblies was going to be harder than I thought.

My conversation with the house assembly leaders went late into the night. I sketched out the major themes of the letter, tracing the overall line of Paul's logic about salvation being for both Jews and Gentiles, that they both together made up the people of God in the new covenant. They were called to glorify God with one unified voice. Their disagreements over how to honor the holy days and what to eat or drink were keeping them from being one people. We talked about fellowship meals and the Lord's Supper, and both sides agreed to discuss again with their assemblies their previous decision about how to handle these matters of difference.

The nine of us last night had felt cramped together in the small upper floor apartment where Andronicus and Junia lived, especially when I had chilled the atmosphere by bringing up the uncomfortable not-eating-together agreement. Priscilla and Aquila, in contrast, had a ground floor dwelling that doubled as their workshop. Their assemblies could welcome many more people—I estimated that at least twenty-five would fit.

I was helping Priscilla prepare. She packed away her leatherworking tools in their custom pouches and stored them in a nook in the wall. I swept, and she arranged all around the floor the beautiful embroidered cushions she had made. It took both of us to roll up and move their large work-in-progress, a market awning for a craftworker. They had only been in this shop for a few years. When Claudius had ordered the Jews out of Rome because of the disturbance, they had left the capital city for Corinth, where they met Paul and, later, me. When they were finally allowed to return, they had had to build their business—and their assembly of believers—all over again. While the Jews were exiled, a few Gentile followers of the Way had continued meeting together, growing cautiously in numbers. After the Jews had returned, they struggled from the minority position—the Weak—to reintegrate into the assemblies that had taken on a distinctly Gentile feel, where the Gentiles held the position of Strength.

As we finished, two kittens poked their noses into the shop. Priscilla scooped them up and took them around the corner to the staircase where she kept dishes of water and meat for stray animals. Aquila returned from the bakery with bread.

Last night the leaders had decided that the small assemblies would each host a meal before I read the letter. They would let the Jews bring their own food and the Gentiles bring their own food. But at least they would share an eating space together.

The members of Priscilla and Aquila's assembly began to arrive: innkeepers, other leatherworkers from the guild, a few of Aquila's customers of high status, and a few people of no status at all. Most carried food, and my stomach growled. I hadn't eaten much since my meager dinner the night before. Frankly, I had been looking forward to trying the exotic cuisine I had heard about from travelers to Rome.

I smoothed my gown, self-conscious because it was one of my older garments. The sailors on my ship had displaced one of my traveling trunks along the way.

The Gentiles arranged themselves on one side of the room, the nineteen of them taking up more than half the space. The four Jews sat by the hosts. Each group shared their food amongst themselves, but not with each other, and I realized I would have to choose where to sit and what to eat. I was representing Paul, a Jew, and standing in his place. But I was a Gentile, unbound by Jewish food laws, and someone had brought bacon.

Paul could tease me about my internal fire all he wanted; tonight I was glad for it. I needed every bit of strength I could muster. But the flame running up my back, my neck, my cheeks wasn't courage—it was embarrassment, because everyone was looking at me. I very deliberately lowered myself to sit between Priscilla and Tryphaena, bridging the two camps. I chose turnip and radish and goat from the Jews, then I turned to my people. I selected figs in honey and shrimp. Herodion, a distant relative of Paul, wrinkled his nose at me. I turned away from him. Forget his condescension, I was going to get me some of that bacon.

I didn't taste a bite of it. That was the most uncomfortable meal of my life. When it was finally over, I closed my eyes and slumped my head. I hoped the letter would vindicate my odd choices. I wiped my fingers on a small piece of bread and rinsed them in the perfumed water bowl.

When I stood with the letter, prepared to read, I took a few slow, deep breaths. I pictured my friend Paul, short and stooped, standing in front of me. "Again," he would say. And I would read the section again. He would correct my posture, my gestures, my inflection. "Not like that, like this:" and he would demonstrate the way I should perform that line. The conversations and debates, the laughter and the arguments, the money and the love we had poured into this letter had all come to this moment.

I looked into every pair of eyes in the room. I breathed in the authority Paul had given me and the power of the Holy Spirit, and I began to read: "From Paul, a slave of Christ Jesus, called to be an apostle and set apart for God's good news. God promised this good news about his Son ahead of time through his prophets in the holy scriptures."

An hour in, I was regretting my choice to read it without a break. I had to use the latrine quite badly, and my throat was parched. We had never done the whole thing without a pause in the rehearsals. But I was afraid to stop, because if they started asking questions now, we'd never finish, and I was just getting to the best parts. "Welcome the person who is weak in faith—but not in order to argue about differences of opinion. One person believes in eating everything, while the weak person eats only vegetables. Those who eat must not look down on the ones who don't . . ." I watched the few Jews sit up straighter and look at the Gentile crowd, seeming happy that Paul was defending them.

". . . and the ones who don't eat must not judge the ones who do . . ." Now it was the Gentiles' turn to lift their shoulders and look at the Jews.

"God has accepted them *all*," I said. The two groups started whispering amongst themselves, but I ignored them and continued.

When I finally reached the greetings, I sighed with relief. Each one smiled when her or his name was mentioned. Taking the time to include so many had been worth it. They were remembered. They were noticed. They mattered to Paul. "May the God of peace be with you all. Amen," I concluded. I sat down, ready to answer questions.

The first came from one of the Jews. "What does it mean, 'place ourselves under the authority of the government'? What governing authorities? The synagogue officials or the municipal leaders? Or . . . Caesar?"

I did not foresee sleep in my future. I called for drinks and refreshments and excused myself for that latrine break before I tackled this one.

I repeated the scene the next night in the household of Narcissus. Tryphaena and Tryphosa welcomed me. In this meeting, there were no Jews at all. The meal was everything I had hoped for; I relished the decadence. But the conversation turned judgy. Assuming I would take their Gentile side, several women complained about Jewish followers of Jesus who criticized their elaborate meals.

"I agree that nothing is wrong to eat," I told them, "but you're focusing on the wrong things. The kingdom of God is not about eating, but about peace in the Holy Spirit!"

After I read the letter, many of their questions centered around asking me to explain various aspects of Jewish history and practice. Without Jews in their regular meetings, these Gentiles were not as well informed as those who met with Priscilla and Aquila or Junia and Andronicus. I was glad for Paul's thoroughness in preparing me.

When we were done, I stepped away from the crowd and studied a fresco on the wall. It surrounded an inset shelf that held the household idols. How interesting to worship God in this place that was also used to worship other gods. The householder did not believe in Jesus, but he had found that his family members and slaves who did believe became easier to manage, so he allowed their practice and their gatherings.

"Miss Phoebe, may I speak with you?"

I glanced down at the wiry young woman who had appeared at my elbow. Her voice was quiet but clear. I had seen her during dinner carrying platters to the table and noticed how she moved with poise. "Yes, of course."

She tipped her head to motion for the doorway to the garden courtyard of the villa. When I nodded, she turned toward the door. She waited for me to walk through first, then she followed me. I sat down by the fountain. I hoped the splashing water would obscure our voices enough to make her comfortable.

She sat next to me and twisted her fingers in her lap.

"What's your name?" I asked her.

"I am . . . called Rhodine."

"I didn't ask what they call you. What's your real name?"

She scrutinized my face, as if determining whether I was safe. "Sabina."

"Greetings in the name of Jesus, Sabina. What can I do for you?"

"Miss Phoebe . . . the way they listen to you . . . the men, I mean . . . it's . . . I've never seen anything like it. How do you do it?"

"How do I do what?"   "How do you get them to listen to you? I understand that your money—" She stopped and widened her eyes.

I laughed. "You can speak honestly to me. I know that my money gives me status."

"Yes. It's more than that, too, though. You have this . . . presence. And your words carry power."

"Ah, yes, my fiery opinions, Paul calls them."

"People listen to them. They do what you say."

"Well, I think that has to do with the authority Paul has given me to speak for him."

She shook her head. "You read in the letter about the gifts. Prophesying, encouraging, giving, leading. I think you have that gift—leadership."

Paul and Timothy had said the same. I had the gift of leadership, and that's why my church had made me a deacon. That's one reason Paul sent me to Rome. "Yes, you're right. The Holy Spirit has given me that gift to build up the church."

She leaned in closer. "I think I have that gift too."

From the bold way she was speaking to me, I believed her. "Why do you think so?"

"Miss Tryphaena lets me come out of the kitchen for the assemblies because I'm so interested, but the other slaves have to stay behind. Every week I go back to them, and I teach them what I learned. I pray for them. Some of them believe in Jesus now."

Astounding. She wasn't just a leader, she was a church planter.

"Sabina, that's wonderful. You *are* a leader—because people are following you!"

"But not all the people. Not free citizens. Not men."

"The assembly welcomes the gifts of everyone. Tryphosa was telling me that slaves have even shared prophecies in the assemblies."

She waved my words away with her hand. "Slave girls who prophesy? There's a whole marketplace full of them. That's nothing new. It's even a stereotype. But slaves who *lead*? In a church with their *owners*? How could such a thing ever happen?"

She was trusting me, and I decided to trust her. "It happened to me."

"What do you mean?"

"I was a slave."

Her forehead wrinkled upward, and her mouth opened.

"I was a household slave. I showed an ability for management, and I grew into a position as household manager. I worked hard, and I earned money on the side. Enough to buy my freedom. I kept working until I had enough to give away."

"So I have to buy my freedom before I can lead?"

"No," I said. "I started helping and teaching in the assembly in Corinth while I was still a slave. Priscilla herself mentored me."

"But did your owner ever take orders from you?"

I remembered what Junia had told me. "In the Way, a leader is a servant, not a commander. It's not about giving orders. It's not about earning status and honor. Lead by serving, just like you're doing. Don't stop. Don't ever stop." I felt the Spirit stir my heart, and I laid my hands on her head. "Don't you ever give up. You run after Jesus with all you've got, and you will find other people running after you. And don't quit, even if your assembly never recognizes the gift God has put in you. You just keep leading, even without a title."

She rubbed away the dampness on her cheeks. "Thank you," she whispered, and then she darted away, back inside.

I made my rounds of the assemblies, then I met with the leaders again. We talked through how they could work out Paul's advice in each of their groups, then I left them for a few weeks to tend to my other business. I came back one evening in time for the assembly meeting at Priscilla's place.

Several were missing. Three or four fewer Gentiles, and one or two fewer Jews. I asked her, "Where is Herodion?"

She closed her eyes. "He decided to go back to the synagogue. He is very angry that we supported Paul's position that all foods are permissible. He called us covenant breakers."

Tears stung my eyes. Paul would be so sad to hear this.

Those who remained, however, were jovial. The room hummed with excitement and conversation. As they gathered to eat, Tryphaena came in, and with her was the gifted Sabina, who grinned at me. Tryphaena said, "We heard you would be back tonight, Phoebe. We didn't want to wait until you came to our home tomorrow to see you!" After the previous meeting at Narcissus's home, I had had a long talk with Tryphaena about God's upheaval of our social structures, pouring out the Spirit on all people, welcoming slaves as siblings, so I was delighted to see her arrive with Sabina.

The Jews sat interspersed among the Gentiles this time. I watched curiously as they began to eat. Some Jews kept to their own food, while others tasted some of the Gentiles' food and offered their own. One Gentile arrived without his own food and sat near Aquila to eat kosher with him. I moved around the room, greeting everyone and tasting everything.

After the fellowship meal, I took the bread. It was darker than what my household back in Cenchreae could afford, rough and hearty. I thanked God for it, then I called to Sabina. I handed the loaf to her. She said what she had heard me say, which I had heard Paul say: "On the night he was betrayed, the Lord Jesus took bread. After giving thanks, he broke it, saying, 'This is my body which is for you. Do this in remembrance of me.'" She lifted the loaf toward the sky then tore it in half and placed it back on the tray. She ripped off a small piece and went to her owner. "Tryphaena, the body of the Christ, broken for you." The wealthy woman received the bread and ate it.

Sabina served me, saying, "Phoebe, the body of the Christ, broken for you." My nose prickled, and my eyes fogged over. I examined the bread. Broken for each of us, pieces from the same loaf. Members of the same body.

Bibliography
for "Our Sister Phoebe"

"Behind the Name: Ancient Roman Names." Accessed October 16, 2017. https://www.behindthename.com/names/usage/ancient-roman.

Bible, Common English. *CEB Common English Bible—eBook*. Common English Bible, 2010.

Blount, Brian K., Cain Hope Felder, Clarice J. Martin, and Emerson B. Powery, eds. *True to Our Native Land: An African American New Testament Commentary*. Minneapolis: Fortress Press, 2007.

Bruce, F. F. "Some Roman Slave-Names." *Proceedings of the Leeds Philosophical Society: Literary and Historical*. Section 5, Part I (1938): 44–60.

"Food in the Roman World." Ancient History Encyclopedia. Accessed October 17, 2017. https://www.ancient.eu:443/article/684/food-in-the-roman-world/.

Gaventa, Beverly. "Listening to Phoebe Read Romans." Presented at the 21st Susan Draper White Lecture Series, Minneapolis, March 12, 2012.

Jewett, Robert, and Roy D. Kotansky. *Romans: A Commentary*. Edited by Eldon Jay Epp. Second Impression edition. Minneapolis: Fortress Press, 2006.

Käsemann, Ernst. *Commentary on Romans*. Eerdmans, 1994.

Keck, Leander E., ed. *The New Interpreter's Bible Commentary Volume IX: Acts, Introduction to Epistolary Literature, Romans, 1 & 2 Corinthians, Galatians*. Nashville, Tennessee: Abingdon Press, 2015.

Lancaster, Sarah Heaner. *Romans: A Theological Commentary on the Bible*. Louisville, Kentucky: Westminster John Knox Press, 2015.

Oakes, Peter. *Reading Romans in Pompeii: Paul's Letter at Ground Level*. Minneapolis: Fortress Press, 2013.

Witherington III, Ben. "Joanna: Apostle of the Lord—or Jailbait?" *Bible Review* 21 (2005): 12–14.